GEORGIA'S

❧ LIGHTHOUSES AND HISTORIC

COASTAL SITES

Kevin M. McCarthy

Illustrations by William L. Trotter

 Pineapple Press, Inc., Sarasota, Florida

D1209247

Inquiries should be addressed to:
Pineapple Press, Inc.
P.O. Box 3899
Sarasota, Florida 34230

LIBRARY OF CONGRESS
CATALOGING IN PUBLICATION DATA

McCarthy, Kevin.
    Georgia's lighthouses and historic coastal sites / Kevin M. McCarthy : illustrations by William L. Trotter. — 1st ed.
        p.   cm.
        Includes bibliographical references and index.
        ISBN 1-56164-143-X (alk. paper)
            1. Historic sites—Georgia—Atlantic Coast. 2. Atlantic Coast (Ga.)—History, Local. 3. Atlantic Coast (Ga.)—Guidebooks.
    I. Trotter, William L. II. Title.
    F292.A74M37 1998
    975.8'00946—dc21   97-32695
                                                       CIP

First Edition
10 9 8 7 6 5 4 3 2 1

Design by Carol Tornatore
Printed in Hong Kong

$\mathscr{C}$ONTENTS

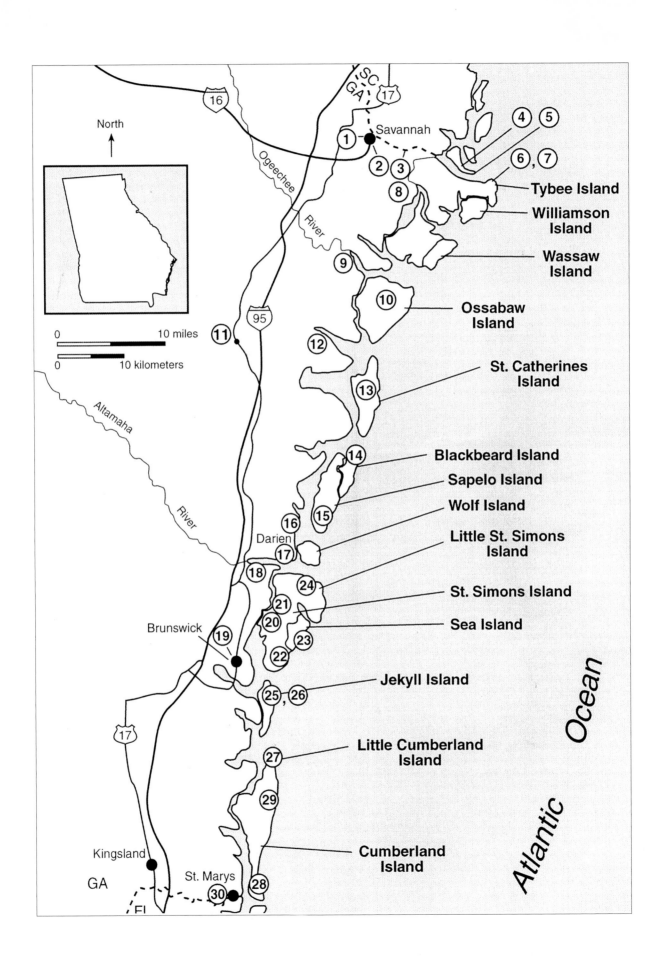

North

Ogeechee River

16

95

11

Altamaha River

17

Brunswick

19

Darien

16

17

18

24

21

20

23

22

25, 26

27

29

28

30

Kingsland

St. Marys

GA

Fl

SC
GA

17

1

Savannah

2 3

8

9

10

12

13

14

15

4 5

6, 7

Tybee Island

Williamson Island

Wassaw Island

Ossabaw Island

St. Catherines Island

Blackbeard Island

Sapelo Island

Wolf Island

Little St. Simons Island

St. Simons Island

Sea Island

Jekyll Island

Little Cumberland Island

Cumberland Island

Atlantic Ocean

0   10 miles

0   10 kilometers

Introduction

Legend has it that a Spanish missionary, working on Cumberland Island in 1595, tried to convince the Spanish king to concentrate on settling Georgia rather than Florida because, ". . . everything was so superior on the Georgia coast." The Spanish king must have disagreed, since he spent much effort and money to establish St. Augustine and missions in La Florida. But today, many people might agree with that Spanish missionary.

Later, as the last-settled and poorest of the original thirteen colonies of the United States, Georgia was caught between the English colonies to the north and the Spanish to the south. Many colonists did not want to declare independence from an England that had supported Georgians for years. How Georgia struggled against foreign forces (the English, French, and Spanish) and established its own independence and identity is part of this book's story.

There are several ways to drive through coastal Georgia. I-95 will speed you on your way, whizzing you past exit signs that hint at what treasures lie off the superhighway. U.S. 17 will take you into the small towns like Midway and Darien. The even smaller east-west roads will take you toward the islands and into towns that lie along the coast of Georgia, the sites that this book highlights.

Years ago, signs along Georgia roads implored you to "Stay and See Georgia." Too many tourists were speeding south to Florida or north to the Carolinas and Virginia. Now, thousands of travelers have discovered the richness of the Peach State. In particular, more and more visitors are attracted by the spectacular beauty of the coast and its long and varied history.

The Georgia coast is a mere 110 miles long, but there is a wealth of natural, historic, and man-made beauty that lies in that expanse between the Savannah and St. Marys Rivers. That thin strip of land has been inhabited for over 4,500 years, but only in the last two hundred years has it seen a great influx of people. But Georgia, learning from the mistakes that other states have made, has done a commendable job in preserving much of its natural coastal beauty, especially that of its sea islands.

Over the years, many Georgians, determined to save their islands and rivers from rapacious developers, have established protected areas, allowed the federal government to control others, and passed strict laws to limit growth.

The "Golden Isles" were so called by gold-seeking Spanish explorers in the 1500s because of the islands' beautiful sandy beaches and sunny weather. Today, these barrier islands face many demands from environmentalists, who want to preserve them for the wildlife; from developers, who want to build near the beautiful unspoiled beaches; and from government officials, who want to leave something for future generations. After researching the history of these islands over the past few years, I am confident that the state is on the right path to reach a balance between development and preservation. Georgia will have many unspoiled, spectacular sites to pass on to future generations.

Writing about Georgia's coastal sites has been one of my most enjoyable research experiences. Climbing the spiral staircase of the Tybee Island Lighthouse or biking around the island, marveling at the engineering skill that built Fort Pulaski, walking through the earthworks of Fort McAllister with no one else around, tracing the footsteps of early settlers down the streets of the abandoned Fort Frederica, and discovering the isolated pockets of mansions all along the coast have given me many memorable moments.

I dedicate this book to the countless Georgians who spurned the quick buck of the developer for the sacrifices that would enable countless visitors to enjoy this state's beauty. All of us who appreciate that natural heritage thank those Georgians.

Among the people I wish to acknowledge for help with this book are Elizabeth E. Arndt, John Breen, Cullen Chambers, F. Warren Murphey, Bill Rivers, Julian Smith, Scott W. Smith, Amy Stewart, Merry Tipton, Bob Wyllie, and especially Buddy Sullivan.

❧ A Short History of Coastal Georgia

You can tell a lot about the history of coastal Georgia by looking at its islands. From north to south, we have Tybee, Wilmington, Skidaway, Wassaw, Ossabaw, St. Catherines, Blackbeard, Sapelo, Wolf, Little St. Simons, St. Simons, Sea, Jekyll, Little Cumberland, and Cumberland. These barrier islands protect the hundred-mile-long Georgia coast. They also have a long, rich history.

The sea islands have protected the Georgia mainland from hurricanes, tidal fluctuations, even Yankee gunboats. Several of the islands (Tybee, St. Simons, and Sea) have been developed. Others (Sapelo, Jekyll, and Cumberland) have some human habitation, but development is tightly controlled. The rest of the islands have been allowed to return to nature: undeveloped, pristine, natural.

The early human history of the islands includes the Native Americans, although little remains of their presence. Either they lived in such close harmony with the land or else the explorers and settlers who followed them destroyed all traces of them.

The Spanish arrived in 1525, but what they found certainly discouraged them: ticks, chiggers, gnats, all kinds of biting insects, and deadly snakes; wilting humidity and heat; dense forest and impenetrable swamp.

We do know from their records that when the Spanish landed on these islands, they found a Native American people that they called the Guale (pronounced "wally"). The name may come from the Spanish pronunciation of the Indian word *wahali*, meaning "the south." The Native Americans belonged to the Muskogean tribe and were related by language to the Creek Nation. Spanish missionaries from St. Augustine, Florida, established missions on some of the islands, with varying degrees of success.

What really changed the history of the coast

was the arrival of the English in 1733. The English Crown wanted to establish Georgia as a buffer between the colonies to the north and Spanish Florida to the south. General James Oglethorpe, leading a group of 114 men, women, and children, landed on Yamacraw Bluff at what would become Savannah. One of the main reasons for Oglethorpe's success in establishing an English presence was the kindness and help given by Tomochichi, a Yamasee leader who welcomed the English and helped them.

Among Oglethorpe's many decrees in establishing the new colony was his outlawing of slavery and rum as two evils Georgia did not need. Later generations would change that rule.

The English laid out Savannah with streets in a grid, a pattern that is still evident today in what many consider one of the South's most beautiful cities. Savannah grew and prospered until the Union blockade during the Civil War isolated it from much of the rest of the country. General William Sherman spared the city, so much of its antebellum architecture remains to this day.

Savannah and coastal Georgia, both of which depended on slave labor to build a strong economy, struggled after the Civil War to recover and begin anew. Labor-intensive crops like rice and cotton gave way to heavy industry, factories, and fishing.

Jimmy Carter's election to the White House in 1976, and Atlanta's becoming one of this nation's most important cities represent a success that few would have predicted for Georgia two hundred—or even a hundred—years ago.

Coastal Georgia has benefited from a strong national and state economy, of course, but it has also produced a remarkable number of farsighted individuals intent on preserving the past and making sure that future generations can enjoy some of this country's most beautiful islands.

How the coast has suffered natural and man-made disasters, how individuals have been able to restore historic forts and buildings, and how thousands of residents and visitors are now discovering the Golden Isles are all part of this book's story.

$\mathcal{O}$NE

✣ First African Baptist Church

Savannah

I have a few books, some good old authors and sermons, and one large bible that was given to me by a gentleman; a good many of our members can read, and are all desirous to learn.
— George Leile, early leader among African Americans in Savannah

$\mathcal{J}$ust west of Franklin Square, between Montgomery Street and Martin Luther King, Jr., Boulevard, stands an important site in the history of Georgia's thousands of African Americans, the First African Baptist Church. The congregation, members of one of this country's oldest African-American churches, began meeting during the American Revolutionary War, survived the Civil War and Reconstruction, and helped lead the way during the Civil Rights Movement of the 1960s. The survival of the congregation is a testament to the faith of its founders and the determination of many of its members over two hundred years of troubled history.

The colony's original founder, James Oglethorpe, had tried to legislate slavery out of Georgia. However, white plantation owners, many of them oblivious to the pain and suffering brought on by slavery, introduced it as a way to work their lands.

Thousands of African Americans can trace their origins back to the isolated coastal plantations on Georgia's

barrier islands, where they were landed from West Africa in chains. One of the enduring legacies of those African Americans is the Gullah/Geechee culture and language, a rich mixture of African, European, and American customs and dialects.

The church is located just to the west of Franklin Square, named for Benjamin Franklin, who served as the Georgia colony's agent in London from 1768 to 1775. Franklin sent samples of Chinese rice from London to Savannah, which helped establish the colony's rice culture. In 1775, as Postmaster General, Franklin established a postal service to deliver the mail in towns from Maine to Savannah. (He is also remembered for helping establish the Bethesda Home for Boys. See Chapter 8.)

The First African Baptist Church traces its beginnings to a British officer's servant, George Leile, also known as George Sharp (c. 1751–?). Around 1773, a white Baptist minister, Matthew Moore, converted Leile and taught him to read. Leile then began ministering to other slaves on the Savannah River plantations. One such place was the Brampton Plantation, which was owned by Jonathan Bryan, an enlightened white man who provided religious services for his slaves.

Leile's master, Henry Sharp, eventually freed Leile, who then preached to whites and blacks around Savannah and spread the Word of God. While the British occupied Savannah during the Revolutionary War (1778–82), they allowed the slaves some freedom, so Leile began holding services for the city's African Americans. When American troops later recaptured Savannah in 1782, the British left and slavery resumed. Leile emigrated to Jamaica, where he founded Baptist congregations and a free school.

The assistant he left behind, Andrew Bryan (1737–1812), continued Leile's work. Bryan had been allowed to preach by Jonathan Bryan, his slave master, a man who had been greatly influenced by the growing presence of the Methodists in Georgia. The date of Andrew Bryan's ordination, January 20, 1788, is considered the founding date of the First African Baptist Church.

In working to buy his freedom, Bryan used some of his own money to buy land for the church he hoped to build. He eventually convinced a number of slaves to spend their day of rest building the church. Bryan's congregation joined the Georgia Baptist Association in 1790 and, together with some smaller white churches, founded the Savannah Baptist Association in 1802. Another early black church in Savannah, Bryan Baptist Church, was also established to serve the growing black population.

As more and more people joined Andrew Bryan's church, it became so large that a number of the parishioners broke away in 1802 to establish the Second African Baptist Church on the east side of Savannah, and then Ogeechee Baptist Church in 1803.

The pastors of the different churches remained on good terms, especially since members of the same families often went to different churches. For example, the wives of three of the deacons of the First African Baptist Church belonged to the Second Baptist Church. The tradition of divided religious loyalties among families also led to a number of mixed marriages in Savannah among Catholics and Protestants in the black community.

Despite the fact that over 65% of the Baptists in Savannah were black, white officials harassed the blacks and limited their active involvement in church activities. For example, only white ministers were allowed to preach at night services, which severely limited such services among blacks. And groups of seven or more slaves were not allowed to assemble for any purpose, other than funerals, without a white person being present.

When Andrew Bryan died in 1812, his nephew, Andrew Marshall, a free black male, became the pastor of the predominantly slave congregation at First African Baptist and helped it to continue its growth. In the 1830s, parishioners organized the country's first black Sunday school there. The church also had the first black-owned brick building in the state. In 1859, the congregation built the present sanctuary (now listed on the National Register of Historic Places) and added a hidden room in the basement to conceal runaway slaves.

The First African Baptist's congregation

continued to grow during Reconstruction and cele-brated its centennial in 1888.

Pastor Andrew Marshall became so popular that he is said to have baptized almost four thousand people. The plantation owners around Savannah, who were pleased with his efforts and with the effects of his work among the slaves, sometimes invited him to preach and perform funeral services in places quite distant from Savannah. While many white people attended his sermons and honored him, other whites were jealous of his building a two-story brick house and tried to have him whipped. Further, the white officers of the Baptist association had to represent the black congregations in legal cases. Such instances as these underscored the fact that black churches need-ed white patronage to remain in existence.

More recently, during the Civil Rights Movement of the 1960s, the First African Baptist Church and other black churches in Savannah helped organize African Americans to boycott downtown businesses until those businesses agreed to hire and serve blacks. The large hall of the First African Baptist provided an important site for mass meetings and planning sessions. These efforts result-ed in the desegregation of the schools, hospitals, libraries, movie houses, and beaches.

Much of what the congregation has suffered in the last two hundred years is documented today in a museum in the church.

Other significant places in Savannah's African-American history include the Beach Institute (502 East Harris Street), which was built by the Freedmen's Bureau in 1867. The Beach Institute was the first school for African Americans in the city, and now has cultural exhibits. The King-Tisdell Cottage Museum (514 East Huntingdon Street) houses exhibits about African Americans. The Laurel Grove-South Cemetery (at the west end of 37th Street) was dedicated in 1852 for the burial of "free persons of color." The Ralph Mark Gilbert Civil Rights Museum (460 Martin Luther King, Jr., Boulevard) includes exhibits of the struggle for civil rights in Savannah. Finally, there is the Nicholsonboro Baptist Church (13310 White Bluff Road, about nine miles south of the city), which was founded in 1868 by two hundred former slaves from St. Catherines Island.

Visitors can learn more about the history of African Americans in Savannah by taking the Negro Heritage Trail Tour, sponsored by the King-Tisdell Cottage Black History Museum and the King-Tisdale Cottage Foundation. For more infor-mation, call (912) 234-8000 or write The Negro Heritage Trail Tour, 502 East Harris Street, Savannah, GA 31401. Admission fee.

DIRECTIONS

The church is located at 23 Montgomery Street, just west of Franklin Square and east of Martin Luther King, Jr., Boulevard.

Further Reading

Janet Duitsman Cornelius. *"When I Can Read My Title Clear": Literacy, Slavery, and Religion in the Antebellum South.* Columbia, SC: University of South Carolina Press, 1991, esp. pp. 21–22.

John W. Davis. "George Liele [sic] and Andrew Bryan, Pioneer Negro Baptist Preachers." *The Journal of Negro History,* vol. 3, no. 2 (April 1918), pp. 119–127.

Georgia Writers' Project. *Drums and Shadows: Survival Studies among the Georgia Coastal Negroes.* Athens, GA: University of Georgia Press, 1986

Gary Wray McDonogh. *Black and Catholic in Savannah, Georgia.* Knoxville, TN: University of Tennessee Press, 1993.

Robert E. Perdue. *The Negro in Savannah, 1865–1900.* New York: Exposition Press, 1973.

TWO

 Trustees' Garden and Pirates' House

Savannah

Of [Long John] Silver we have heard no more. That formidable seafaring man with one leg has at last gone clean out of my life.
— Robert Louis Stevenson, *Treasure Island*

General James Oglethorpe and his small band of colonists came ashore in 1733 close to where the present-day city hall is located in Savannah, near Bull and Bay streets. To settle his group in Savannah, one of Oglethorpe's many activities was his establishment of an experimental garden on the outskirts of the settlement, which he named "Trustees' Garden" in honor of the men back in England who had supported his efforts. The garden's boundaries were the Savannah River on the north, old Fort Wayne on the east, present-day Broughton Street on the south, and present-day East Broad Street on the west. A plaque there calls it the ". . . first public agricultural experimental garden in America."

In 1734, workers built a small gardener's house nearby. That building, which is close to today's Pirates' House, may be the oldest house in Georgia. The gardener used the front section of what is called the "Herb House" for his tools and his office, used the back room for his stable, and the upstairs for the hayloft. The bricks to build the house were made a short distance away near the Savannah River.

Modeled after London's Chelsea Botanical Garden, the ten-acre garden experimented with many different types of plants to see which would do best in the Georgia climate. Botanists from England sailed off to many different countries, especially South America and the West Indies, to gather plants for the experimental garden.

The English authorities had hoped to make Georgia not only a buffer between the twelve colonies to the north and Spanish Florida to the south, but also a productive food supplier. After all, Georgia had the most temperate climate and longest growing season of the thirteen American colonies. If Georgia could produce what England was importing at great expense, it would more than pay for itself and also provide a good income for the new settlers.

Because many in England believed that food cultivation in Georgia would not entail much work, slavery was prohibited. The Trustees had planned to populate the colony with free white laborers from the lower classes of Europe, including England. Those men would be indentured servants who would produce crops for the land owners and eventually earn their own freedom. Native American slaves were sometimes begrudgingly allowed and some Georgia plantation owners surreptitiously kept a few black slaves, but in general the prohibition of slavery was enforced in the first few years of the colony. However, that prohibition would not last very long.

Gardeners in Savannah were soon cultivating cotton, flax, hemp, indigo, medicinal herbs, and different spices. The gardeners tried to cultivate oranges, but the soil and climate were not suitable for the citrus trees. Two other crops for which officials had high hopes were grapes for a wine industry and mulberry trees for a silk industry. Oglethorpe's own high hopes are revealed on the original Georgia seal, which had a mulberry leaf, a silkworm, and a cocoon with the words "Non sibi sed aliis," which means "Not for ourselves but for others."

In anticipation of beginning a silk industry, Oglethorpe had brought with him Paul Amatis, an Italian silk producer who later took charge of the Trustees' Garden. Other Italian families followed, all hopeful of establishing a silk industry in Georgia.

The silk producers later built in Savannah a public filature, a place where silk is reeled. Today, a plaque in Reynolds Square commemorates that filature.

In 1751, the Trustees, still thinking that silk would be a viable product in Georgia, decreed that the only men who could be members of the assembly that was meeting in Georgia to decide the fate of the colony were those who were cultivating one hundred mulberry trees and producing fifteen pounds of silk a year for each fifty acres of land they owned. That decree had little effect, however, since the Trustees gave up control of Georgia to the king in 1752.

Both the grape and mulberry crops failed because of various conditions beyond the power of those early farmers. The wine turned out to be poor quality, and the mulberry trees that grew wild in Georgia proved unappetizing to the silkworms. But at least Oglethorpe and his farmers had tried to make those two crops viable.

Two notable successes, however, were the peach tree and the cotton plant, both of which would bring much-needed income to both Georgia and South Carolina in the decades ahead. However, such a shift from the original plans of the Trustees, which had stressed the cultivation of silk and wine, led some plantation owners to push for the use of slaves. Their insistence would later lead to much soul-searching and eventually to the widespread use of slavery.

In the 1750s, when there was no longer a need for the experimental garden, officials converted the garden site, building an inn to serve the needs of the many sailors who came to the bustling seaport. Tradition says that among the law-abiding sailors were pirates and other bloodthirsty brigands who drank, caroused, and fought in the area. Stories have persisted over the years about the many drunken seamen who were shanghaied at the inn. Thus the Pirates' House began.

Taverns like the original Pirates' House served many purposes in Savannah. They were places where banquets could be held, where citizens could congregate with government officials in a convivial atmosphere, where alcohol consumption could be controlled to some degree, and where travelers could find lodging. If some taverns, especially those near the waterfront, deteriorated and became the haunts of pirates, many others remained respectable.

The modern Pirates' House has tried to preserve much of the ambience of those early days in its interior design. The Captain's Room, for example, has handhewn ceiling beams. A story persists that a tunnel led from under this room through the Rum Cellar to the docks and served as a quick way to drag drunken sailors on board ships. However, the tunnel has not yet been found.

Robert Louis Stevenson is said to have set part of his famous novel, *Treasure Island*, at this inn. Some say the novel's infamous Captain Flint died in an upstairs room and that his ghost roams through the hallways. Today, pasted on the walls of the restaurant are pages from early editions of *Treasure Island*.

Whether pirates ever frequented the Pirates' House is anybody's guess. What is certain is that pirates did indeed roam the Georgia coast. The infamous Blackbeard, for example, had an island named after himself (see Chapter 14). Chances are that pirates did come into Savannah in the eighteenth century, since it was a leading cotton port and attracted many sailors, both good and bad.

DIRECTIONS

The Pirates' House is located near the intersection of East Broad and Bay Streets. Phone: (912) 233-5757.

Further Reading

Harold E. Davis. *The Fledgling Province: Social and Cultural Life in Colonial Georgia, 1733–1776*. Chapel Hill, NC: University of North Carolina Press, 1976.

Robert Louis Stevenson. *Treasure Island*. New York: Charles Scribner's Sons, 1911.

Betty Wood. *Slavery in Colonial Georgia, 1730–1775*. Athens, GA: University of Georgia Press, 1984.

HREE

✣ Fort Jackson

Savannah

Fort Jackson—may it prove as firm a defense against, and a great terror to, the enemies of American liberty, as was a firm patriot whose name it bears.
— The seventh of seventeen toasts drunk during a celebration in 1809

The insect repellent offered in the ticket shop at Fort Jackson testifies to what life must have been like there 230 years ago. Jackson, Georgia's oldest standing fort, dates back to the Revolutionary War, when soldiers loyal to the colonies built a battery, referred to in official papers as a "mud fort," on what had been a brickyard on the south bank of the Savannah River. However, even before the battery could fire its first shot, an outbreak of malaria forced the troops to evacuate.

The fort is on Salter's Island, named for an early owner of the island, Thomas Salter. When Salter died in 1751, his stepson, William Harris, continued working the mill and rice plantations that were operating there. The location of the island—on the Savannah River and near the ocean—was ideal for shipping his products elsewhere, including to the growing settlement of Savannah to the west.

During the Revolutionary War, officials realized how vital the site was, since it controlled the shipping lanes of both the main channel and the back river, through which all boats entering Savannah's harbor had to pass. Military strategists, especially those who did not have to remain at the site and fight the mosquitoes, appreciated the island's natural topography, especially the marshes that protected the fort from land attack and the deep anchorage offshore. That anchorage, called "Five Fathom Hole," facilitated the loading and unloading of troops and supplies.

When British troops occupied Savannah in 1778, in an effort to block the channel and prevent the French from attacking the city by sea, they deliberately sank several of their own vessels opposite the fort. So successful were the British in defending Savannah from French and American assault that, despite being outnumbered three to one, the British routed the attackers.

In that assault, the Americans lost one of their greatest allies, Count Casimir Pulaski, who was killed in the battle. He would be honored in the naming of Fort Pulaski on Cockspur Island (see Chapter 4).

When the British finally surrendered in Savannah in 1782, the American officer who accepted their surrender was James Jackson, for whom the fort was named. He later served as a brigadier general in the state militia, member of the U.S. House of Representatives (1789–91), U.S. senator (1793–95, 1801–06), and governor of Georgia (1798–1801).

In 1808, President Thomas Jefferson drew up plans for a widespread system of forts to guard the American coastline from possible attacks by British or French ships. American officials, who by then had acquired the island for military purposes, assigned Captain William McRee, a teenager who had graduated from West Point three years before, to build a fort on Salter's Island. His workers were able to complete a brick battery, wooden barracks, and powder magazine before the beginning of the War of 1812.

During the building of the fort, part of which was done by slave laborers, James Madison was elected president of the United States. On March 4, 1809, a dinner party was held at the fort to commemorate the election, and some seventeen toasts were drunk to various people and events. Among these was the toast that opens this chapter. In 1819,

President Monroe visited the fort during a stay in Savannah.

Until 1827, the fort also functioned as the major quarantine inspection station of the area. Between 1845 and 1860, workers added a moat, drawbridge, more barracks, privies, a rear wall, and another powder magazine.

The fort remained relatively quiet until the outbreak of the American Civil War. The Georgia militia seized Fort Jackson in 1861, and when Union troops captured Fort Pulaski in April of 1862, Jackson became a part of the main defense system for Savannah. The great Robert E. Lee, who at one point commanded the coastal defenses of Georgia and South Carolina, inspected the fort that year. Noting its deteriorating condition, he ordered that earthworks be built nearby. The presence of Confederate troops at Fort Jackson, as well as eight earthen batteries or forts near Fort Jackson, prevented Union naval forces from attacking Savannah.

The commander of the Confederate forces in Savannah, Edward Clifford Anderson, had served for several terms as the city's mayor before the war (a post he held immediately after the war as well). So well did Anderson know the area that he was able to run the nearby Union blockade in 1861 with what may have been the Confederacy's largest single shipment of war supplies.

When General Sherman captured Savannah in 1864 at the end of his infamous "March to the Sea," Anderson led his troops to safety across the river into South Carolina. Soon after, the C.S.S. *Savannah* fired on the Union-occupied fort, apparently the only time when a Confederate ironclad ship fired on a Union-held masonry fort.

After the end of the Civil War, officials renamed the site "Fort Oglethorpe" to honor Georgia's great founder, James Oglethorpe. This name remained until 1905, when the War Department gave the name Oglethorpe to an active military base in north Georgia and restored "Jackson" as the name of the Savannah site.

In 1965, the Georgia Historical Commission acquired Fort Jackson, had an access road to the fort built, and made plans for establishing a maritime museum there.

Today, the nonprofit, private Coastal Heritage Society maintains the fort and the museum, which is part of the inner fort. Among the exhibits are cannons, including a thirty-two pounder that is the largest muzzle-loading cannon still being fired in the United States. The Savannah Chapter of the United Daughters of the Confederacy cooperates with the Coastal Heritage Society to demonstrate the thirty-two pounder cannon for the public.

The gift shop and entrance to Old Fort Jackson is the former post–World War I Tybee Train Depot, which was barged to the site in 1988. The depot was once the departure point for train rides to Tybee Island between 1887 and 1933, but the opening of the highway to the beach in 1933 made the train unnecessary.

A red buoy in the river marks the site of the wreck of C.S.S. *Georgia,* the state's first ironclad built during the Civil War. The vessel was deliberately scuttled by evacuating Confederates during the fall of Savannah. She had been stationed downriver from Fort Jackson as a floating battery. The vessel has suffered considerable damage, but it is still a remarkable survivor of the 1860s.

DIRECTIONS

Fort Jackson Historic Site is located just north off U.S. 80 (Islands Expressway) about three miles east of Savannah. Hours: 9 A.M.–5 P.M., Monday through Sunday. Admission fee. Phone: (912) 232-3945. A self-guided tour takes about one hour.

Further Reading

Forts Committee, Department of Archives and History. "Fort Jackson." *Georgia Magazine,* October-November 1968, p. 17 and ff.

Alexander A. Lawrence. *A Present for Mr. Lincoln: The Story of Savannah from Secession to Sherman.* Macon, GA: Ardivan Press, 1961.

Richard McMurry. "Sherman's Savannah Campaign." *Civil War Times Illustrated,* vol. 21, no. 9 (January 1983), pp. 8–15.

William N. Still, Jr. *Savannah Squadron.* Savannah, GA: Coastal Heritage Press, 1989.

Thomas L. Stokes. *The Savannah.* New York: Rinehart & Co., Inc. 1951.

❧ Fort Pulaski

Cockspur Island

I am here to defend the fort, not to surrender it.
— Colonel Charles Olmstead, when first asked to surrender
the Confederate stronghold of Fort Pulaski in 1862

As you drive to Fort Pulaski along a road lined with oleanders and palmettos, then enter the well-manicured grounds of the silent fortification, it is hard to imagine the terror and hellish noise of artillery shells landing inside the fort on that fateful day in 1862 when military engineering changed forever.

The fort is located on Cockspur Island, considered by many invading forces to be the key to the control of Savannah and much of interior Georgia. British forces, for example, set aside twenty acres on the island for harbor fortifications, as did the United States federal government.

The first fort on the island, Fort George, was a colonial blockhouse. Fort George was built in 1761 to protect Savannah, especially from attacks by the Spanish stationed in St. Augustine, Florida. When that threat ceased, officials used the facility for quarantine and customs inspections.

At the start of the Revolutionary War, two British ships arrived, intending to secure both fresh supplies and information from refugees on what was happening in Georgia. At that time, the island had become a haven for the loyalists who escaped there from American troops. One of those fleeing from Savannah was Sir James Wright, the royal governor. Because he had with him the great seal of the province, for a short time Cockspur Island became the capital of colonial Georgia.

In 1794, workers built a second fort on the island, Fort Greene. The idea was to protect the southern flank of the new republic. However, a severe hurricane destroyed the structure ten years later.

The present fort was part of the coastal fortification system adopted after the War of 1812. Work did not begin on it until 1829, when Robert E. Lee, then on his first military assignment after graduation from West Point, designed and built the drainage system and dikes. Work continued until 1847. During that time, some twenty-five million bricks were laid; piles were driven into the marsh to support the huge structure resting on the deep mud of Cockspur Island.

Officials named the fort after Revolutionary War hero Casimir Pulaski (1748?–79), who had died in the Battle of Savannah (October 1779) and was either buried at sea near Cockspur Island or interred in what later became the Pulaski Monument in Savannah's Monterey Square.

At the start of the Civil War in 1861, members of the Georgia militia seized the pentagonal fort and later turned it over to the Confederacy. The following year, federal forces, as part of their plan to blockade the southern coast, moved into the vicinity and prepared to seize the fort. They stationed themselves on nearby Tybee Island, abandoned by the Confederates on the advice of their leader, Robert E. Lee, who thought it could not be defended. Under the cover of darkness, the federals began building eleven batteries with which they began bombarding Fort Pulaski in April 1862.

The Confederate soldiers thought the fort, with its seven-and-a-half-foot-thick walls, impregnable. But the men had no way of knowing that the federal troops, for the first time in the history of warfare, were using a new type of weapon, rifled cannons that were able to penetrate the masonry walls.

The Confederate commander, Colonel Charles Olmstead, at first had stated, "I am here to defend the fort, not to surrender it." When he realized that the shells were falling closer and closer to the powder magazine, he reluctantly decided he could no longer hold the fort. He surrendered after just thirty-one hours of bombardment. Olmstead later tried to justify his decision:

> We were absolutely isolated beyond any possibility of help from the Confederate Authorities, and I did not feel warranted in exposing the garrison to the hazard of the blowing up of our main magazine—a danger which had just been proved well within the limits of probability. . . . There are times when a soldier must hold his position "to the last extremity," which means *extermination*, but this was not one of them.
> – *Fort Pulaski Official Map and Guide*

From then on, engineers had to design and build new types of forts to counteract the rifled artillery.

Once the fort fell, the federals repaired the breached walls and used the facility as a stronghold, effectively preventing the Confederate forces from using Savannah as a seaport. The blockade of Savannah was so tight that whatever goods remained in the city became very expensive and in short supply.

When Union General William T. Sherman eventually reached Savannah in December 1864, after burning his way through much of eastern Georgia, the Confederate troops still in the city left to fight battles elsewhere. The mayor surrendered the city to the Union troops, hoping to spare Savannah from the Union torch. At that point, General Sherman sent his famous telegram to President Lincoln:

> To His Excellency—
> President Lincoln.
> Dear Sir—
> I beg to present you as a Christmas gift, the City of Savannah with 150 heavy guns and plenty of ammunition; and also about 25,000 bales of cotton.
> W.T. Sherman, Maj. Genl.
> [*A Present for Mr. Lincoln*, front matter]

For the most part, the Union soldiers behaved themselves honorably. In their letters home, they praised the city as the most beautiful place they had ever seen. They particularly liked Monterey Square and its impressive monument to Count Pulaski. A photograph taken of a group of soldiers at Fort Pulaski in 1862 or 1863 shows a baseball game being played in the background. (Some scholars claim that photograph is the oldest known photograph of the game being played.)

Today, visitors to the fort can see the Civil War fortifications, the seven-foot-deep moat, the drawbridge and heavily fortified entrance, cannon on top of the walls, and various storerooms under the walls. While much of the bombardment damage was repaired by Union troops in 1862, officials have left some damage to show visitors the intensity of the attack. You can still see in the pockmarked walls a few of the holes left by the five thousand Union shots fired at the fort.

Brief taped messages at audio stations within the walls explain the different uses of the fort. In the summer, rangers give talks throughout the day. Several trails lead through the coastal marsh for a closer look at the aquatic life around the fort. A small monument in the area commemorates the 1736 visit of John Wesley, the founder of Methodism.

DIRECTIONS

To reach Fort Pulaski, follow the signs along U.S. 80. The National Park Service operates the fort, which is open daily except for Christmas, 8:30 A.M.–5:15 or 6:45 P.M., depending on the season. Special events are held on the weekend nearest the anniversary of the siege of the fort (April 10–11), Labor Day, near Christmas, and at other times. Write or call for a schedule. Phone: (912) 786-5787. Admission fee.

Further Reading

Q.A. Gilmore. *Siege and Reduction of Fort Pulaski, Georgia.* 1862. Reprinted: Gettysburg, PA: Thomas Publications, 1988.

Conoly Hester. "Will Pulaski's Bones Ever Find Peace?" *Georgia Journal*, November/December 1996, p. 8.

Allen P. Julian. "Fort Pulaski." *Civil War Times Illustrated*, vol. 9, no. 2 (1970), pp. 8–21.

Ralston B. Lattimore. *Fort Pulaski National Monument, Georgia.* Washington, D.C.: U.S. Department of the Interior, 1954.

Alexander A. Lawrence. *A Present for Mr. Lincoln: The Story of Savannah from Secession to Sherman.* Macon, GA: Ardivan Press, 1961, esp. pp. 51–65: "The Brick Fort and the Rifled Cannon."

John A. Mitchell. "Convincing Test for Rifled Cannon" [about the fall of Fort Pulaski]. *Military History*, July 1987, p. 12 and ff.

Herbert M. Schiller. *Sumter Is Avenged! The Siege and Reduction of Fort Pulaski.* Shippensburg, PA: White Mane Publishing Co., 1995.

Rogers W. Young. *Robert E. Lee and Fort Pulaski.* Washington, D.C.: United States Department of the Interior, 1941, National Park Service Popular Study Series, History No. 11.

$\mathcal{F}$IVE

$\sim$ Cockspur Island Lighthouse

Cockspur Island

I shook off the dust of my feet and left Georgia, having preached the Gospel there (not as I ought, but as I was able) one year and nearly nine months.
— John Wesley, who first landed in America on Cockspur Island in 1736

After a three-hundred-mile trip from the Appalachian Mountains to the northwest, the Savannah River empties into the Atlantic Ocean. On its way, it passes around Cockspur Island and forms a natural boundary between Georgia and South Carolina.

Cockspur Island, which is within sight of the Atlantic and guards the two entrances into the Savannah River, takes its name from the shape of its dangerous reef, which projects out into the open water. Despite the fact that little of the island lies above the high-water mark, this small piece of land has played an important role in coastal Georgia's history.

In 1733, General James Oglethorpe passed by the island with his band of settlers as they made their way twenty miles up the river to establish Savannah at Yamacraw Bluff. It was here, three years later, that John Wesley (1703–91), the father of Methodism, first set foot in America.

Just off the eastern end of the island, in the south channel of the Savannah River, is a little knoll that was the site of the Cockspur Island Lighthouse, also known as "Little

Tybee Light." First built in 1849 and then rebuilt in 1857 on the foundation of the first tower, the structure stands sixteen feet wide at the base and rises forty-six feet. On the ocean side, an angled wall breaks the force of incoming waves. On a clear night, ships some ten miles away at sea could see the fourth-order Fresnel lens beaming its warning light.

The lighthouse keeper, who lived on the much drier Cockspur Island, made daily trips to the Cockspur tower to maintain the wick, service the lamp, clean the window panes, and polish the lens. The first lighthouse keeper (1849) had the appropriate name of John Lightburn. Long after Fort Pulaski was abandoned, the lighthouse keepers stayed on at the fort. They had to move to higher ground, however, when the hurricane of 1891 put the fort's parade ground five feet under water. After the hurricane, workers built the lighthouse keepers a two-story house on top of the fort.

Several of the lighthouse keepers suffered or died at the site. For example, the second keeper, Cornelius Maher (1851–53), drowned at the site when his boat capsized. His widow, Mary Maher, was appointed to take his place (1853–56), a practice common in those days when the widows of light-keepers had no other means of support.

In 1855, Mary Maher may have witnessed a tragic event near the fort. Two men, John Chaplin of South Carolina and Dr. Kirk of Savannah, although related by marriage, had such a fierce dispute over something that they agreed to fight a duel to settle the matter. Chaplin fired the first shot, but aimed it high in the air, perhaps to show that he really meant no harm to his brother-in-law. But Dr. Kirk refused to follow suit. Instead, he fired at Chaplin, wounding him in the foot. Chaplin became so angry that he fired at Dr. Kirk and killed him.

The man who replaced Mary Maher in 1856, Thomas Quinfiven, survived only four months before fever killed him. The son of lightkeeper Patrick Eagan drowned offshore when their boat capsized on their way to light the beacon. Yet another keeper, Charles Poland, had his house on Cockspur Island struck by lightning in 1880. The hurricane of 1881 blew away what remained of the keeper's house.

Cockspur Island Lighthouse, built long after the nearby Tybee Lighthouse of 1736, was paired with another small lighthouse on Oyster Bed Island in the North Channel of the Savannah River. The Oyster Bed Island Lighthouse, however, did not survive the storms that buffeted the area.

During the fierce bombardment of Fort Pulaski by Union forces on Tybee Island, the Cockspur Island Lighthouse managed to survive (see Chapter 4). Although the lighthouse stood in the direct line of fire, the shells passed overhead, and the battle was over so quickly that there was no damage to the tower.

The keeper who began working at Cockspur Island Lighthouse in 1881, George Washington Martus, had a sister, Florence (1868–1943), who was born at Fort Pulaski on Cockspur Island. She became famous as the "Waving Girl," faithfully greeting every ship that entered the harbor near their home on Elba Island.

Having waved for some forty-four years to those who were arriving or leaving Savannah by ship, she had endeared herself to thousands of people. Her waving inspired a number of theories about why she did it. Some speculate that she had vowed to a sailor she had fallen in love with that she would greet every ship that passed her island until he returned—which he never did. Few people ever met her, but she became the subject of romantic legends in ports all around the world. She was honored when a Liberty Ship, built in Savannah in 1943, was named for her. There is a statue of her on River Street near the waterfront in Savannah, and a plaque commemorating her at Fort Pulaski near the visitors' center.

In 1909, when the large ships sailing to Savannah began using the deeper North Channel, Cockspur Island Lighthouse was finally deactivated. In 1949, the Coast Guard abandoned the lighthouse, which is now part of Fort Pulaski National Monument. The National Park Service took it over in 1958. The little tower, which has withstood over 100,000 high tides in its existence, was restored in 1960, 1978, and 1996.

DIRECTIONS

Cockspur Island Lighthouse is off the eastern end of the island in the South Channel of the Savannah River. Visitors to the lighthouse should go there only by boat, since at high tide the water rises to the base of the tower, which sits on an oyster bar. For most people, the best place to see the lighthouse is from the walls of Fort Pulaski or Lazaretto Creek Bridge.

Further Reading

Margaret Godley. *Historic Tybee Island.* Tybee, GA: Tybee Museum Association, 1958, 1985, esp. pp. 37–40 [about Florence Martus, Savannah's "Waving Girl"].

Buddy Sullivan. "The Lighthouses of Georgia." *The Keeper's Log: The Quarterly Journal of the United States Lighthouse Society,* vol. 4, no. 3 (Spring 1988), p. 5.

$\mathcal{S}$IX

$\mathfrak{so}$ Tybee Lighthouse

Tybee Island

Tybee Island was ". . . a Place so exceedingly pestered with Musketoes, by Reason of the adjacent Marshes, that no Person would ever be fond of taking his Abode there."
—William Stephens, representative of the Trustees of the Georgia Colony in the eighteenth century

$\mathcal{B}$ecause Tybee Island guards the major sea entrance to Savannah, General James Oglethorpe, when he founded the colony in 1733, wanted to put a beacon on the island to guide ships to and from the settlement. To build the lighthouse, Oglethorpe selected William Blithemann as master carpenter. Oglethorpe moved ten families to the island and gave each a fifty-acre lot. However, the mosquitoes were so bad that several of the settlers died before the octagonal tower was finished, a tragedy that some of the people of Savannah mistakenly attributed to overindulgence in rum.

At one point, Oglethorpe was so upset at the lack of progress on the beacon that he jailed the master carpenter and threatened to hang him. The carpenter's crew pleaded for their boss's life and promised to finish the tower within five weeks. In the next sixteen days, they completed more work than they had done in the preceding sixteen months. In 1736, the men finally finished the ninety-foot-tall wooden tower, supposedly the tallest building of its kind in America at that time.

The only problem was that the structure was too close

to the sea and therefore subject to beach erosion. After a storm washed away the first tower in 1741, officials had the workers begin a new stone-and-wood tower, which they finished in seven months. The man in charge of the construction that time, Thomas Sumner, was so successful with the new tower that he was able to petition English officials for five hundred acres of land near Frederica on St. Simons Island to the south, plus six indentured servants. This eventually made Sumner a rich man.

Despite Sumner's pride in the tower, he too had built it too close to the ocean, which soon threatened to topple it. In 1773, workers built much further inland a third, one-hundred-foot-tall brick lighthouse with interior wooden stairs and landings. Like its predecessors, it did not have a light. Instead, it was to be used only as a daymark. The tower finally acquired its first lantern in 1789, two years after the establishment of the U.S. Lighthouse Service.

In 1822, workers built a second, smaller tower to seaward and installed a fixed light so that mariners could line up the two towers to determine where the channel was. During the Civil War, retreating Confederate forces, concerned that the bright light would aid approaching Union troops, succeeded in putting the lighthouse out of commission by removing the lens and setting the stairs on fire. After the federal troops landed, they used Tybee Island to bombard Fort Pulaski and force it into submission.

From 1820 until 1860, the nearby land close to the Martello Tower had another use. The area became the favorite dueling site of South Carolinians, whose strict laws in their own state outlawed duels. Wronged gentlemen intent on defending their honor and settling disputes would row over from South Carolina, knowing full well that they would not be prosecuted for dueling in the state of Georgia.

In 1866, after the Civil War had ended, officials had workers build a new brick and cast-iron lighthouse. The new tower used the lower sixty feet of the octagonal third lighthouse, to which builders added ninety-four feet. A first-order Fresnel lens was placed at the top. (That light still shines

today. On a clear night, it can be seen from eighteen miles at sea.)

Work on the new tower was delayed when federal troops unwittingly brought cholera onto the island, killing the foreman and four workers. It would take another year for the work to be completed by the Lighthouse Service.

When the light first shone on October 1, 1867, the tower was all white. Twenty years later, the bottom half of the tower was painted black, the upper half white. It is still possible to see the cracks in the tower wall caused by storms and an 1886 earthquake. In 1933, electricity replaced the kerosene that had been used to fuel the light.

In the nineteenth century, Tybee Island became a popular recreational area, even though visitors had to reach it by sailboat or steamer. When a railroad was built in 1887 from Savannah to the island, many Savannah residents made the day trip for picnics and swimming.

Tybee Island's Fresh Air Home has also served as a haven for children. Begun in 1898 with a budget of $100, the Fresh Air Home was at first a convalescent home for children with respiratory and other physical problems. Later, it became a summer vacation spot for city children. It can accommodate one hundred children every two weeks.

Today, the seventy thousand annual visitors see on the five-acre site the tower (which can be climbed for a spectacular view of the surrounding counties), the houses of the Headkeeper, First Assistant Keeper, and Second Assistant Keeper, and the original summer kitchen and fuel storage building. Georgia's oldest, tallest lighthouse is maintained by the nonprofit Tybee Island Historical Society.

The island today is a favorite with visitors and residents alike, as is clear from the many year-round homes, summer cottages, and condominiums. The island is in fact one of the most developed barrier islands in Georgia, and has the only beach on the state's northern coast that is accessible by road.

Two other nearby sites should be mentioned here. These are Tybee National Wildlife Refuge and Williamson Island. The Wildlife Refuge is a one-hundred-acre sandbar at the mouth of the Savannah

River, and is best seen from a boat rather than on foot. The sandbar is a spoil disposal site, used by dredgers contracted by the U.S. Army Corps of Engineers. It is a favorite spot for many kinds of birds, including nesting terns.

Williamson Island, just south of Tybee Island, northeast of Wassaw Island, and east of Little Cabbage Island, is very new, having been formed over the past several decades. Williamson began as a sand spit off Little Tybee. It gradually became an island, growing to some 250 acres in the mid-1970s before erosion and new channels took away half the sand. The island is named after the late Jimmy Williamson, former mayor of Darien, Georgia, and a member of the State Board of Natural Resources.

Hermit crabs, ghost crabs, and many shore-birds inhabit the island. Its rapid formation and subsequent change in shape, especially after strong northeasters, have made it clear that boat owners have to be very wary when navigating among the barrier islands.

Further Reading

Margaret Godley. *Historic Tybee Island*. Tybee, GA: Tybee Museum Association, 1958, 1985.

Alexander A. Lawrence. *A Present for Mr. Lincoln: The Story of Savannah from Secession to Sherman*. Macon, GA: Ardivan Press, 1961.

Buddy Sullivan. "The Lighthouses of Georgia." *The Keeper's Log: The Quarterly Journal of the United States Lighthouse Society*, vol. 4, no. 3 (spring 1988), pp. 2–11.

Richard W. Wittish. "A Railroad Revival" [about the Tybee Island Railroad]. *Savannah Magazine*, vol. 7, no. 5 (September/October 1996), pp. 29–33.

DIRECTIONS

To reach Tybee Lighthouse, drive east on U.S. 80 to Tybee Island. Follow signs to "Historic Tybee Lighthouse and Museum" on the northern part of the island. Turn left on Campbell Avenue and drive two blocks. Turn left on Van Horne Street and continue one block to Meddin Drive. Turn right on Meddin and you will see the lighthouse. Hours for admission: 10 A.M.–6 P.M. daily in the summer; 12 noon–4 P.M. on weekdays and 10 A.M.–4 P.M. weekends in the fall and winter. Phone: (912) 786-4077 or (912) 786-5801.

SEVEN

❧ Fort Screven

Tybee Island

However small, it at least keeps me away from office work and high theory.
— Lt. Col. [later Army Chief of Staff] George C. Marshall, on
being assigned to Fort Screven

The Georgia coast is defended by a series of barrier islands. These islands protect the mainland to some degree from the hurricanes that roar in from the Atlantic, and also minimize erosion by the ocean, winds, and storms. The islands are very susceptible to weather patterns (hurricanes, winds, rain, drought) and human involvement (do we develop the islands or leave them alone?). They have diverse environments, ranging from tidal marshes, creeks, and rivers on their west sides to beaches and dunes on their east sides, facing the Atlantic. The west sides also have waterways that provide birds, fish, and people a safe inland passage or, depending on one's loyalties, a way to attack coastal cities.

Tybee Island, located at the northeastern tip of Georgia's coast, is one of the best-known of the barrier islands. Its name may come from the Native American Euchee word for salt or from the name of the Choctaw chief, Iti Ubi, or from "tabby," the material that coastal settlers used to build their homes. Although only two-and-a-half miles long and two-thirds of a mile wide, its location at the mouth of the

Savannah River has made it an important defense post for the past two hundred years, as well as a resort area for visitors and a home to many permanent residents.

The area to the west of the island has a site that is unknown to many of those who frequent the beaches and tourist sites. When a 1749 Georgia law allowed slaves to be imported, authorities established a hospital, called a "lazaretto" from the Italian word for pest-house. Here, particularly sick people arriving in Savannah by ship were confined and treated. Those who died there were buried in unmarked graves. Later, the facility, which is memorialized in the name of nearby Lazaretto Creek, became a slave hospital, where owners left their sick slaves. If the slaves recovered, their owners would sell them in the slave market in Savannah. If the slaves died, they were buried in the nearby unmarked graves.

Much of the military history of Tybee Island revolves around Fort Screven on the northeast coast of the island. Screven sits on a strategic location that effectively guards the approaches to Savannah. At various times in its history, the site was controlled by the Spanish, the French, the British, the Confederacy, and the Union. Its strategic position allowed Union soldiers to bombard Fort Pulaski and reduce its massive walls to rubble (see Chapter 4).

After the Civil War, officials realized that a fort positioned on the tip of Tybee Island was essential for guarding the approaches to Savannah, so they began making plans to build one. They wanted to incorporate in the new fort the latest design findings from battles fought in similar sites. For example, the knowledge that engineers gained from the bombardment of Fort Pulaski, namely that masonry and brick forts could not withstand a shelling by rifled-bore cannon, resulted in the use of dirt and sand on the outer walls of the batteries at Fort Screven.

It took much time and planning to complete the fort. During its building, the fort's name changed from Fort Tybee to Fort Graham and finally to Fort Screven. This name honors General James Screven, a Georgia native who was killed in action in 1778 near Midway, Georgia, during the Revolutionary War.

The U.S. Army Corps of Engineers first acquired the property in 1875. However, work on the fort did not begin until 1897, after the coastal defense system had been revised and engineers had designed new structures that incorporated the lessons learned during various wars. The main difference from earlier forts, which used compact fortifications, was that the new fort had low, concrete batteries with walls up to twenty feet thick, and sand coverings of several dozen feet in front of the concrete walls. This made the walls almost invisible among the dunes.

Workers finished the first of six batteries in 1898 (and the rest of the fort seven years later), placing in it guns with a range of seven or eight miles. At that time, America and Spain seemed destined to fight a war over Cuba, especially after the sinking of the U.S. battleship *Maine* in Havana harbor with the loss of 266 American lives. Thus, engineers fortified Georgia's coastal defenses, especially the entrances to Savannah, Darien, Brunswick, and St. Marys harbors. Savannah's presumed vulnerability and Fort Screven's important location led to the strengthening of the fort.

When there was no longer a Spanish threat to the southeastern United States, officials found another use for Fort Screven. It became the headquarters for the antisubmarine forces that this country marshalled against German U-boats in the two world wars. Because those vessels could threaten East Coast ports, the harbors of Savannah, Georgia, and Charleston, South Carolina, had to be fortified.

The fort remained in active use as the Fort Screven Reservation until 1945. Over time, it added facilities for families, for example, an elementary school for the children of civilian and military personnel. It also served as a training site for coastal artillery National Guard units; as an infantry post; and as a school for deep-sea diving.

Among the many distinguished officers who saw duty at Fort Screven was George C. Marshall, who served as the commanding colonel in 1932. During World War II, he became the U.S. Army Chief of Staff, and the architect of what became known as the Marshall Plan for rebuilding Europe

after the war. General Marshall also won the 1953 Nobel Peace Prize.

After World War II, when the fort became one of many that were no longer needed in peacetime, the federal government sold it to Savannah Beach for $200,000. A year later, the town sold off much of the fort's three hundred acres to local developers, who transformed the officers' quarters into beautiful houses.

Today, the memories of thousands of soldiers stationed at Fort Screven in World War II bring them back for visits. Some of those soldiers, who enjoyed their assignment at the fort and its proximity to the ocean and beaches, returned after their military careers to settle down with their families. Others come back for vacations.

Near the ocean and overlooking the former parade ground, there remain some of the two-story homes where the officers lived. Although most of the other remnants of the military presence are gone, the museum inside Fort Screven has exhibits on the history of the fort and of Tybee Lighthouse and Tybee Island.

DIRECTIONS

As you enter Tybee Island from the west on U.S. 80, turn left onto Campbell Avenue and follow the signs. The museum is opposite Tybee Lighthouse. The museum is open daily 10 A.M.–6 P.M. in the summer, 1–5 P.M. in the winter. Phone: (912)786-4077.

Further Reading

James Mack Adams. *A History of Fort Screven, Georgia.* Tybee Island, GA: JMA2 Publications, 1996.

Tonya D. Clayton, Lewis A. Taylor, Jr., et al. *Living with the Georgia Shore.* Durham, NC: Duke University Press, 1992.

Fort Screven (1897–1945): A Tour of Georgia's Historic Coastal Fort. Tybee Island, GA: Tybee Museum Association, 1988.

Margaret Godley. *Historic Tybee Island.* Tybee, GA: Tybee Museum Association, 1958, 1985.

Charles Rippin. "The Guns of Tybee: Exploring Ft. Screven." *Coastal Quarterly,* vol. 2, no. 1 (no date), pp. 16–19.

*E*IGHT

✍ Wormsloe State Historic Site

Isle of Hope

Wormsloe is one of the most agreeable Spots I ever saw, and the improvements of that ingenious Man are very extraordinary.
— Edward Kimber in 1744

*W*ormsloe is the site of an early tabby home of one of the first European settlers in Georgia. The avenue leading to what is now Wormsloe State Historic Site, which begins at a stone arch, is one of spectacular beauty. Stretching for a mile and a half, the road is lined with over four hundred live oaks, the state tree of Georgia. The trees on each side of the dusty road touch overhead, and seem to lead visitors into an earlier time when plantations were isolated and self-sufficient.

When General Oglethorpe and the Trustees were making plans for establishing the new colony of Georgia, they wanted to bring in the poor and persecuted people of Europe. The plan was for the colonists to produce enough goods on the land to support themselves and at the same time, benefit the colony's supporters in England, including the king. The settlers would also help defend against the Spanish in Florida, who claimed Georgia for themselves.

Despite Oglethorpe's original plans to take many poor people with him on the first trip across the Atlantic, in the end he chose mostly laborers, merchants, and tradesmen, although as many as one-third of those first settlers may have

been destitute. They finally reached their destination in February 1733. Among the 114 passengers on the *Anne* was the Jones family: husband Noble, a physician and carpenter from Surrey, England, and his wife Sarah, son Noble Wimberly, and daughter Mary.

Oglethorpe gave many of the settlers plots of land within the new city of Savannah, but gave others land outside the city so that they could produce crops and help protect the city from foreign forces. Those who established private plantations outside Savannah were given larger plots of land. They were able to take advantage of the rich coastal plain, and could more easily experiment with different crops, for example, citrus trees, mulberry trees for silk manufacture, and grape vines.

One of those who eventually chose to live and work outside Savannah was Noble Jones. He was assigned to patrol the Georgia coast with a group of select rangers, but was also responsible for using the militia to stop a particularly dishonest man, Thomas Bosomworth, from using local Native Americans to destroy Savannah in 1749 (see Chapter 13 for more about them).

Four years after arriving in the colony and applying for a lease of five hundred acres on what came to be called the "Isle of Hope," Noble Jones began to clear the dense forest, plant crops, and build the tabby house at the center of Wormsloe (sometimes spelled "Wormslow") Plantation. The "tabby" house, so called because it was made of sand, lime, and oyster shells, is one of the very few structures that survives from Oglethorpe's period.

Located on one of the inland approaches to Savannah, the Wormsloe fortified house helped control one of the waterways to Savannah. At that time the Inland Waterway was the main north-south route in the colony. By the time it was finished around 1744, the building had one-and-a-half stories and five rooms encircled by an eight-foot-high enclosure. Bastions at each corner of the house allowed those inside to cover all approaches.

Jones had a distinguished career in early Georgia. He served as constable, as town surveyor for Augusta and New Ebenezer, and for eighteen years as

a member of the Royal Council. As the years went on, the Jones men, father and son, differed as to whom they supported in the American push for independence. The father remained loyal to his king. But the son, Noble Wimberly Jones, who had become a doctor and planter, supported independence. The father died in 1775, a year before the colonies declared independence. His son, who would go on to serve in the Second Continental Congress, eventually passed the Wormsloe property on to his heirs. Descendants have lived in a nearby private house ever since. Near the house and overlooking the salt marsh are the graves of the Noble Jones family.

During the Civil War, Confederate troops built fortifications and a large earthen battery in the area, the remains of which are still visible on the grounds. Called Fort Wimberly, the fortification also protected the inland waterway to Savannah.

The museum on the grounds and the exhibits around the site describe Jones's colonial estate. Artifacts excavated on the grounds, as well as a video about the founding of Georgia as the thirteenth colony, give a multifaceted approach to the site. From time to time "Living History" demonstrations show visitors what life was like in the area two hundred years ago.

DIRECTIONS

Take Exit 16 from I-95 and go twelve miles on State Road 204 (Abercorn Street) toward Savannah. Take a right onto Montgomery Crossroads and go 3.2 miles until you reach an intersection. Turn right onto Skidaway Road and go 0.8 miles to the entrance of the site. Phone: (912) 353-3023. Open year round; Tuesday–Saturday, 9 A.M.–5 P.M.; Sunday, 2 P.M.–5:30 P.M. Closed on Mondays, New Year's Day, Thanksgiving, Christmas Day. Admission fee.

*T*hree other nearby notable sites include the Bethesda Home for Boys, which is two-and-a-half miles from Wormsloe. An orphanage, it has also taught non-orphans over the years. The school was founded in 1740 by the colony's fourth Anglican pastor, Rev. George Whitefield, a dedicated administrator who spent much of his career raising funds for the school. He was even able to convince the usually tight-fisted Benjamin Franklin to donate generously. The institution, which is supposedly the oldest continuously operated orphanage in this country, had to be made self-sufficient. So Whitefield and his successor, James Habersham, thought that slaves should be allowed to do the menial labor at the orphanage, which sat on five hundred acres of good farmland. Whitefield and Habersham were therefore partly responsible for the fact that slavery was instituted in Georgia in 1749.

DIRECTIONS TO BETHESDA FROM WORMSLOE

Turn left at the exit onto Skidaway Road, go for one-half mile, turn left onto Ferguson Avenue, go for 2.1 miles, and turn left into the brick-columned entrance of the school. A small museum on the grounds describes life at the school over the years.

The second nearby site is Pin Point, a small African-American community in which Supreme Court Justice Clarence Thomas spent his early years.

DIRECTIONS TO PIN POINT FROM BETHESDA

Turn left on Ferguson Avenue, turn left after one block onto Diamond Causeway, and turn right after 0.6 mile into Pin Point.

The third site is Skidaway Island, on which is the Skidaway Institute of Oceanography and Skidaway Island State Park with campsites, nature walks, and picnic sites. The island is further down Diamond Causeway, which crosses a river 1.3 miles past Pin Point. The river used be called "Back River," but its name was changed to "Moon River" in honor of Savannah native son Johnny Mercer, who composed a hit song in 1961 about a body of water he called "Moon River."

DIRECTIONS TO SKIDAWAY ISLAND FROM PIN POINT

Diamond Causeway leads to Skidaway Island, then into McWhorter Drive. The Institute of Oceanography is at the north end of McWhorter Drive. The institute has a Marine Extension Center with a saltwater aquarium, exhibits, and interpretive programs open to the public. Open 9 A.M.–4 P.M., Monday-Friday; 12 noon–5 P.M., Saturdays. Phone: (912) 356-2496.

Further Reading

Susan H. Albu and Elizabeth Arndt. *Here's Savannah: A Journey through Historic Savannah & Environs.* Savannah, GA: A&E Enterprises, 1994.

E. Merton Coulter. *Wormsloe: Two Centuries of a Georgia Family.* Athens, GA: University of Georgia Press, 1955.

Georgia Writers' Project. "Pin Point" in *Drums and Shadows: Survival Studies among the Georgia Coastal Negroes.* Athens, GA: University of Georgia Press, 1986, pp. 82–88.

William M. Kelso. *Captain Jones's Wormslow.* Athens, GA: University of Georgia Press, 1979.

$\mathcal{N}$INE

$\mathscr{S}$ Fort McAllister

near Richmond Hill

Men go to war to kill or be killed if necessary and should expect no tenderness.
— General William Sherman justifying his order that Confederate prisoners be the ones to remove land mines around Fort McAllister

$\mathcal{T}$he Great Ogeechee, a tidal river that is navigable by ocean-going vessels, flows for 250 miles through Georgia on its way to Ossabaw Sound, where it empties into the Atlantic Ocean. The river almost became one of the most important in the state when, in 1755, Royal Governor John Reynolds chose the centrally located village of Hardwicke on the Ogeechee as Georgia's capital to replace Savannah. The change never materialized and Hardwicke remained small.

However, to the east of the town, a fort was built that was important in the Civil War. On the south side of the first high ground above the mouth of the river, ten miles west of the Atlantic Ocean, the fort is the South's best-preserved Confederate earthwork fortification. It succeeded in keeping Union ships out of the river for much of the Civil War. It defended the "back door" to Savannah, twelve miles to the north, and also protected both the nearby Atlantic and Gulf Railroad bridge, which carried a major supply line to the Confederacy, and the rice and cotton plantations along the river. The structure was named for the Joseph McAllister

family, which owned Genesis Point.

Begun in 1861, a year before the Union capture of Fort Pulaski near Savannah, the fort's design was very different from Pulaski's. Engineers realized that masonry fortifications were not as effective as earthworks, which could more easily absorb punishing bombardments. So workers began using shovels and wheelbarrows to move the great quantities of dirt necessary for the massive walls of the fort, and to dig out the ditch surrounding the fort. Inside the ditch were sharpened stakes to ward off attack from the land side.

Each bomb shelter, a huge, grass-covered mound, had its door facing away from the water to protect it from bombardment from the sea. Visitors can still examine, in at least one of the bomb shelters, a bedroom and storage area.

The fort had to withstand numerous attacks by Union naval vessels, including Monitor-class ironclads, which could bombard the fort with shells that weighed as much as 450 pounds apiece. One of the Union ironclads was *Montauk*, commanded by John Worden, who had also commanded the *Monitor* in her battle with the C.S.S. *Virginia* (formerly the *Merrimack*) off Norfolk, Virginia. What little damage was done to the fort by the Union vessels could be repaired during the night by the Confederates.

One of the fort's main weapons was something called a "hot shot gun," so named because it fired cannonballs that soldiers had heated to red-hot temperatures in a furnace. The idea was that the cannonballs would set fire to wooden ships offshore. However, the big guns inside the fort had a difficult time reaching the Union's ships, which kept at a distance and were using their rifle-barreled cannons effectively.

One of the naval attacks on the fort killed Major John Gallie, Fort McAllister's commander, the fort's only fatality through the naval attacks it endured.

Men inside the fort witnessed the demise of the C.S.S. *Rattlesnake* (previously christened the *Nashville*), a Confederate blockade runner and privateer. When it tried to leave the Ogeechee River and run the Union blockade to take some goods overseas

in return for desperately needed supplies, the *Rattlesnake* ran aground near the fort. Its days were numbered. The Union ironclad *Montauk* proceeded up the river and destroyed the helpless ship.

The Union finally captured the fort not by a frontal assault from the sea, but an attack on the land side by General Sherman's army in December 1864. The fort's defenders were well-prepared for a naval assault, but not for a land-based attack, because the bigger guns could not be turned toward the land. One of the Confederate soldiers wrote home, saying that ". . . a strong place it [Fort McAllister] is, and the Yanks never can take it so long as they knock at the front door." But when the federals attacked from the back door, it took less than half an hour before they overran the defenders and captured the fort.

When General Sherman later confronted Major Anderson, who had replaced Major Gallie as commander of Fort McAllister, Sherman asked him about the land mines, called "torpedoes," that were laid in the area before the fort. (The land mines had wreaked a terrible toll on Union soldiers, killing and maiming many of them.) "Do you condone the use of torpedoes in civilized warfare?" Sherman asked, and Anderson replied, "I was sent to Fort McAllister to obey orders, not to question them." Sherman answered: "It's inhuman. It's barbarous. And this is your 'Southern chivalry.'" Sherman then forced the Confederate prisoners-of-war to remove the mines. This was a dangerous task, but fortunately none of the men were killed. As General Sherman explained: "Men go to war to kill or be killed if necessary and should expect no tenderness." Finally, Sherman's troops burned the fort's bunkers and then abandoned the area.

The fall of the fort forced the residents of unprotected Savannah to flee. Sherman was able to open up communications and a supply route to the sea, thus ending his infamous "March to the Sea."

Henry Ford, founder of the Ford Motor Company, bought Fort McAllister in the 1930s and had much restoration work done on the site.

Henry Ford had other interests in the area besides Fort McAllister. In the 1930s and 1940s, he

provided schools for public education, medical care for the poor, and experimental farms for agricultural research.

He also developed an aquaculture station at nearby Richmond Hill, which experimented with producing different kinds of fish. Today, Richmond Hill Fish Hatchery, which the state of Georgia operates, produces many native fish which it then distributes throughout the state and to other places in exchange for species not usually available in Georgia. The hatchery, which gets many of its female fish from the nearby Ogeechee River, is open to the public. The hatchery is located just off State Road 144 east of exit 15 off I-95.

One of Henry Ford's friends, inventor Thomas Edison, had a laboratory at a power station on the Ogeechee.

Ford's estate later sold the place to the International Paper Company, which gave it to the state of Georgia in 1958. Workers have since restored the fort to its 1865 appearance and added a museum with exhibits of artillery and artifacts from the Civil War. Among the exhibits is material from the C.S.S. *Rattlesnake*.

Reenactments of Civil War battles take place during the year, for example, during Labor Day weekend and the first weekend in December. The adjacent Richmond Hill State Park has picnic areas, restrooms, and facilities for camping. On the Fourth of July, thousands of people gather at Fort McAllister for a barbecue.

DIRECTIONS

Take exit 15 from I-95, drive east on State Road 144 for 6.4 miles, then onto 144 Spur, and watch for signs to the fort. The fort is open 9 A.M.–5 P.M., Tuesday-Saturday; 2 P.M.–5:30 P.M., Sunday. Phone: (912) 727-2339 or 727-3614.

Further Reading

William E. Christman. *Undaunted: A History of Fort McAllister, Georgia*. Darien, GA: Georgia Department of Natural Resources, 1996.

Alexander A. Lawrence. *A Present for Mr. Lincoln: The Story of Savannah from Secession to Sherman*. Macon, GA: Ardivan Press, 1961, esp. pp. 93–102: "Fort McAllister Versus Lincoln's Navy," and pp. 181–187, "Fort McAllister Again."

Jeffrey Mosser. "Gateway to the Atlantic" [about Union general Sherman and Fort McAllister]. *Civil War Times Illustrated*, vol. 33, no. 5 (December 1994), pp. 62–70.

EN

🔗 Slave Cabins

Ossabaw Island

Ossabaw Island is as wild as any place in Georgia, even the Okefenokee. . . .
– David R. Osier

Ossabaw Island, the northernmost of Georgia's Golden Isles, is now almost totally deserted by humans. As one walks along the nine miles of pristine beaches and examines the salty marshes, it's easy to imagine what it must have looked like to the first European explorers sailing along the coast.

The name of the island, one of the oldest place names in the state, goes back to the Spanish pronunciation of the Native American Guale (pronounced "wally") name in the Creek or Muskogean language, and means "yaupon holly bushes place." The Muskogeans used the leaves of the yaupon holly to make the "black drink" that they used at town meetings. Seminole leader Osceola had a name with the same origins as Ossabaw Island; it meant "black-drink singer." The Spanish called it "Asopo" or "Asapo," and the British spelled it "Ossebau," "Ussawbaw," and "Ussybaw."

Native Americans used Ossabaw Island for thousands of years as a hunting and eating place. Some of the artifacts around the many shell mounds date back four thousand years.

When General James Oglethorpe signed a treaty with Chief Tomochichi, permitting the British to establish a colony in what became Georgia, the treaty reserved Ossabaw, St. Catherines, and Sapelo barrier islands for the Native Americans for hunting. Later, those islands were given to a half-breed Native American, Mary Musgrove, in gratitude for her interpreting for General Oglethorpe (more details in Chapter 13).

John Morel, a successful planter from South Carolina, bought Ossabaw Island in 1760, had his slaves clear the land on the island, and planted indigo for use as a dye. He went on to accumulate considerable wealth from his indigo plantation. During the American Revolution, he supported independence and harbored those fleeing the British. Later, he divided his holdings into three plantations, which his sons inherited. In the early 1800s, his family introduced sea-island cotton to the island.

By the 1850s, other owners controlled the island and had as many as 1,200 African slaves working the land. In 1864, during the Civil War, Confederate Lieutenant Tom Pelot led a force that captured a two-masted Union warship, *Water Witch*, that was lying at anchor in Ossabaw Sound, and used it for patrolling the Georgia coast. Because the Union blockade prevented the ship from using the ocean route to Savannah, the Confederates tried to float her to the city by inland routes, but soon ran aground.

Although the capture of the Union ship did much to raise the spirits of the people of Savannah, eventually General Sherman's "March to the Sea" in late 1864 necessitated that the ship be burned to keep her from being recaptured.

In the early 1900s, wealthy families, such as the Wanamakers of Philadelphia, bought the island as a hunting preserve and introduced hogs, which now number over three thousand. In 1924, Dr. H.N. Torrey of Michigan bought it as a winter retreat and built a huge Spanish-style home on the north end of the island.

In 1961, Eleanor "Sandy" Torrey West, who is the only person still living on the island, together with her former husband, Clifford West, formed the

Ossabaw Island Foundation. That organization began the Ossabaw Island Project. From 1961 through 1982, the Project brought together for retreats artists, musicians, writers, scientists, business people, and many students. In 1978, Ms. West sold the island to the state, which took over the management of the Foundation's programs. A lack of funds eventually ended the many worthwhile projects on the island sponsored by the Foundation.

As Georgia's first State Heritage Preserve (the most restrictive designation for land protection that the state has), the island is maintained by the Georgia Department of Natural Resources as a ". . . wilderness preserve, to be used solely for natural, scientific, and cultural study, research and education, and environmentally sound preservation of the island's ecosystem."

In 1995, the National Trust for Historic Preservation listed this island as one of the nation's eleven most endangered places. The large pink-stucco mansion in the Mediterranean Revival style is deteriorating, as are three tabby slave cabins that were built around 1845. Those slave cabins, remnants of the cabins used by the 1,200 slaves that worked the four plantations on the island, were placed on the National Register of Historic Places in 1996. The island also has two hundred archaeologically significant aboriginal sites.

Visitors, who can arrive only by boat, disembark at Torrey Landing on the north end. There they see a breathtaking view of live oaks that were probably planted in the 1760s by John Morel.

While Ossabaw is now almost totally deserted by humans, it is home to about five hundred alligators, two thousand deer, and more than three thousand hogs. There is even a herd of sixty donkeys, descended from five that were given to one of the boys who lived on the island thirty years ago. Controlled hunts each year eliminate about three hundred each of the deer and hogs, but keeping their numbers down is very hard for the state managers.

What is probably most remarkable about this well-preserved island is that the Torrey family chose to sell it to the state rather than to the better-paying private developers who wanted to build golf courses and condominiums. The island wasn't developed in the early part of this century because wealthy families had bought it as a hunting preserve and did not want high-rises. But by the 1960s, the high property taxes that were forcing those families to sell this and other islands almost forced Ossabaw into the hands of developers.

Instead, the Torrey family and a few others, in order to preserve the island for future generations, decided to sell their holdings, not to the highest bidder, but to the state and federal governments. For eight million dollars, about half of what she could have gotten, Ms. Torrey and her brother's heirs sold Ossabaw to Georgia. She will continue to live on the island, but after her death, the mansion and remaining land will pass to the state.

DIRECTIONS

Because Ossabaw Island is so restricted, visitors are usually not permitted. However, boaters do use the beaches in the summer. Hunters on the five state-controlled quota hunts each year must have special permission from the Georgia Department of Natural Resources.

Further Reading

Joseph R. Campbell. "The Archeology of Eastern Georgia and South Carolina." *Archeology of Eastern United States*, edited by James B. Griffin. Chicago: The University of Chicago Press, 1952, pp. 312–321.

James Cerruti. "Sea Islands: Adventuring Along the South's Surprising Coast." *National Geographic*, March 1971, pp. 366–393.

Betsy Fancher. *The Lost Legacy of Georgia's Golden Isles*. Garden City, NY: Doubleday, 1971, esp. pp. 195–208: "Cumberland, Ossabaw, and Wassaw: The Threatened Wilderness."

Don W. Farrant. *The Lure and Lore of the Golden Isles*. Nashville, TN: Rutledge Hill Press, 1993: pp. 141–145 [about the capture of the *Water Witch*].

David R. Osier. "Ossabaw Miracle." *Georgia Journal*, January/February 1997, pp. 12–24.

H.N. Torrey. *The Story of Ossabaw*. Privately printed, no date.

Burnette Vanstory. *Georgia's Land of the Golden Isles*. Athens, GA: University of Georgia Press, 1956, esp. pp. 10–20: "Ossabaw Island."

ELEVEN

❧ Midway Church

Midway

Her great men are numbered by scores; her influence is felt in thousands of places.

— James Stacy, *History of the Midway Congregational Church*

The large white church on U.S. 17, twenty-five miles south of Savannah and ten miles from the coast, is at the center of what many consider Georgia's "Cradle of Liberty." From this church has come a remarkable number of great citizens: two signers of the Declaration of Independence; six congressmen; four governors; one United States minister to a foreign country; eighty-two ministers, including the fathers of physician and author Oliver Wendell Holmes and telegraph inventor Samuel Morse; six foreign missionaries; several university chancellors; and numerous attorneys, authors, doctors, inventors, scientists, and teachers, as well as many average citizens.

Many of Midway's parishioners are buried in the cemetery across the street. Five Georgia counties were named for Midway men: Baker, Gwinnett, Hall, Screven, and Stewart.

Midway Congregational Church can trace its origins to the English Puritans who arrived in Massachusetts in 1626. Some of them eventually made their way to South Carolina and later, in 1752, to Midway, Georgia. The name of the town referred to the fact that it was halfway between Darien and

Savannah on the stage road. The new arrivals obtained from Savannah authorities land grants totaling 32,000 acres. The first Puritan settlers and their slaves arrived later that year to make their home and begin working the land.

The settlers were Congregationalists who soon attracted three hundred like-minded parishioners. In 1754, some of them organized the Midway Society and erected a church. They also worked hard cultivating rice, indigo, and other crops, and many of them prospered. Midway settlers took an active part in establishing St. Johns Parish in 1758. They also supported the independence of the American colonies at an early point, unlike many other Georgians.

Members of St. Johns Parish, made up of independent-thinking Congregationalists, supported independence so strongly that at one point, because of the reluctance of many Georgians to join them in the independence movement, they asked to be annexed to South Carolina. St. Johns Parish was later renamed "Liberty County" to honor its many colonists who upheld the independence of the new United States.

The reluctance of many Georgians to support the independence movement was understandable, considering how young and poor the colony was, and how much it depended on England to support it economically. When the English Parliament passed the "Intolerable Acts" that closed the port of Boston, Georgia called a meeting of parishes in 1774. But, dominated by older, more conservative citizens with close ties to England, the meeting rejected the idea of sending delegates to the First Continental Congress in Philadelphia.

The Midway people used their church as a gathering place for meetings on independence, which led to the burning of the church in 1778 by the British, who invaded Georgia from Florida. After the Revolutionary War, the Midway Society rebuilt the church, finally completing it in 1792.

The parish prospered until General Sherman passed through in 1864, destroying much property in the area on his "March to the Sea." Union troops vandalized the church and, in fact, used it as a slaughterhouse. As a result of Sherman's destruction of food sources, many of the residents moved elsewhere and never returned. The last official meeting at Midway Church was held in December 1865.

One member who attended services in the church during the Civil War was Matilda Harden Stevens, whose memory of her life in Midway was published in the *Georgia Historical Quarterly* in 1944. Mrs. Stevens, in mentioning that the church had two pastors, neither of whose sermons she usually understood, noted a disturbing fact:

> One day, while the junior minister was preaching, something that he said arrested my attention and I became interested, Subsequently, finding that I always understood him, I became troubled, thinking that I was not spending the day in a spiritual manner, that it was not keeping God's day holy to enjoy anything so much. (Ramsey, p. 277)

Her description of the services, which the family spent the whole of every Sunday driving to and from and attending, showed just how much the community tried to make their religion the centerpiece of their lives.

Members use the church today for weddings and funerals, and for homecomings for the descendants of the original settlers. The Midway Society, a nonprofit organization made up of descendants of the original settlers, has made extensive renovations in the church in an effort to preserve this important part of colonial Georgia. Visitors can tour the church, as well as the cemetery across the road.

Next to the church is the Midway Museum, where visitors can obtain a key to the church. The museum is a replica of an eighteenth-century raised cottage style that was widely used in the area. Among the many exhibits in the building is one of eight known sets of musical glasses popular in the eighteenth century. A guide can play these for visitors.

The cemetery across the road is always open to the public and is well worth visiting for its important grave sites. A monument in the center honors Georgia's three signers of the Declaration of Independence. Two of them (Lyman Hall, who later became governor of Georgia, and Button Gwinnett)

are from St. Johns Parish. There are also the grave of General James Screven, a Georgia native killed near Midway during the Revolutionary War and after whom Fort Screven (see Chapter 7) is named, and the tomb of John Lambert. Lambert, who had been found as an infant in a basket on Lambert's Bridge in South Carolina, was raised by various kindhearted people, and grew up to be a wealthy man. He left his estate for charitable purposes.

It is also possible to find, with the help of a brochure from the museum across the street, the grave of Dr. Abner Porter, the only known suicide in the cemetery. Porter killed himself when he could not decide which of two young ladies he loved more. Because he committed suicide, his body was buried outside the walls. Later, his grave was included inside the grounds when the cemetery had to be enlarged.

A crack in the wall is visible at the northeastern corner of the church, marking where a slave murdered by another slave is buried. Some believe that the spirit of the murdered man keeps cracking the wall to indicate that a crime was committed there.

One mile north of Midway Church on U.S. 17 is Hall's Knoll, the former home of Lyman Hall, signer of the Declaration of Independence, member of the First Continental Congress, and Governor of Georgia.

DIRECTIONS

Midway is 1.6 miles west of I-95 off Exit 13 on U.S. 84/GA 38. The church is 0.4 miles north on U.S. 17. The church is on the right, the museum just beyond the church, and the cemetery across the street.

The Museum is open 10 A.M.–4 P.M., Tuesday-Saturday; 2 P.M.–4 P.M., Sundays. Closed Mondays and all holidays. Admission fee. Phone: (912) 884-5837.

Further Reading

Betsy Fancher. *The Lost Legacy of Georgia's Golden Isles.* Garden City, NY: Doubleday, 1971, esp. pp. 83–100: "Midway Church: Piety and the Christ Craze."

Robert Long Groover. *Sweet Land of Liberty: A History of Liberty County, Georgia.* Roswell, GA: WH Wolfe Associates, 1987.

Josephine Bacon Martin. *Midway Georgia in History and Legend, 1752–1867.* Midway, GA: Midway Museum, 1932, 1958.

Annie Sabra Ramsey, editor. "Church-going at Midway, Georgia as Remembered by Matilda Harden Stevens." *The Georgia Historical Quarterly,* vol. 28, no. 4 (December 1944), pp. 270–280.

James Stacy. *History of the Midway Congregational Church, Liberty County, Georgia.* Newnan, GA: S.W. Murray, 1951.

$\mathcal{T}$WELVE

 Fort Morris

Sunbury

Come and take it!
— Colonel John McIntosh to a superior British force when
asked to surrender Fort Morris

$\mathcal{S}$ome towns dwindle because of economic factors, such as a devastating hurricane, disease, the placement of a railroad, etc. All of these factors contributed to the decline of Sunbury. This little Georgia town had its moment of glory and then simply disappeared into history, to be revived only recently as a resort town. Early in the eighteenth century, this lovely town, located on the western bank of the Medway River ten miles from Midway, rivaled Savannah as a busy seaport. But then came the Revolution, and Sunbury never recovered from its effects. Its decline was due mostly to its close proximity to Savannah.

The Medway River may have been named after sites in England, while the town of Sunbury, whose name literally means "sun town," may have taken its name for its sunny location on the river. Even today, city planners are impressed by the way that the 496 lots and three squares of the original town were laid out in a very orderly fashion, and that all the lots were uniform in size. This is evident from the plan on exhibit in the museum at the visitor center near the fort.

In 1752, Captain Mark Carr obtained a land grant of

five hundred acres at the mouth of the Medway River. Six years later, Carr gave three hundred acres to other settlers from Midway to open a seaport for the planters. Sunbury was established in 1758, and officials built defensive forts to protect it. More defenses were built in 1773. As a port, Sunbury was important to local plantation owners, who preferred using it to ship their rice rather than making the long, expensive, overland trip to Savannah.

Sunbury began to prosper. Naturalist William Bartram visited the town in the mid-1760s and described it as having ". . . pleasant piazzas around [its houses] where the genteel, wealthy planters resorted to partake of the sea breeze, bathing and sporting on the Sea Islands." At that time, the town had some eighty homes and several businesses. And Sunbury was associated with quite a few illustrious names, including all three of Georgia's signers of the Declaration of Independence: Button Gwinnett, Lyman Hall, and George Walton, the last of whom was imprisoned there by the British. Also from this small seaport came three U.S. Senators, one U.S. Representative, and four Georgia governors.

When the American Revolution began in 1775, the Continental Congress decided to build Fort Morris on Georgia's coast to protect the southernmost colony from attack by the British Navy. The Medway River fort, the only Revolutionary War earthworks still remaining in Georgia, was named after a captain who commanded an artillery company there during the Revolution.

The irregularly shaped fort had a surrounding parapet and moat, and enclosed a large parade ground where the contingent of 250 officers and men could march. Two dozen pieces of artillery were positioned to defend the fort from both land and sea attacks. Besides using the fort as a defensive bulwark, American forces used it to launch three unsuccessful invasions of British East Florida during the war.

In November 1778, five hundred British ground troops, backed by armed ships in the Medway River, captured Sunbury. But when the British demanded that Fort Morris surrender, the fort's commander, John McIntosh, although greatly outnumbered, replied, "Come and take it!" For some reason

—perhaps unnerved by the American response or maybe not willing to risk the lives of their own troops—the British retreated. After the conclusion of the war, the grateful Georgia legislature presented McIntosh with a sword inscribed with his famous words.

The British, however, returned six weeks later. American officials ordered the fort's new commander, Major Joseph Lane, to evacuate. He refused to do so, perhaps egged on by the citizens of Sunbury. In the ensuing battle against the larger British force, four American soldiers were killed and seven wounded before the fort finally fell in January 1779. American officials later court-martialed Major Lane for disobeying their orders to evacuate.

After that, Sunbury was burned to the ground. The fort, which the British renamed "Fort George" in honor of King George III, was used as a prison for American officials until the British finally withdrew from Georgia in 1782.

Several citizens of Georgia tried to revive the town after the Revolution. They did succeed in establishing the prestigious Sunbury Academy in 1793, but neither Academy nor town survived.

During the War of 1812, a new fort, Fort Defiance, was built inside the grounds of Fort Morris. It was named in honor of Colonel McIntosh's refusal to surrender to the British in 1778.

The area, however, received the brunt of hurricanes in 1804 and 1824, as well as epidemics of malaria and yellow fever. It was never to regain its former importance. Today near the fort nothing remains of the colonial town of Sunbury.

For many decades, nature was allowed to reclaim the Sunbury area. Finally, in 1968, the Georgia Historical Commission took it over. Officials placed Fort Morris on the National Register of Historic Places in 1971, and later built a visitor center with exhibits about the history of this fascinating place. From the hard-packed earthworks of the fort there is a fine view of St. Catherines and Ossabaw islands, neither of which is open to the public.

Visitors can visit the Sunbury Cemetery, which is the only remaining physical evidence of the

thriving port. Established in 1758 and still showing gravestones dating from 1788 to 1911, the cemetery has thirty-four markers still standing. These include a memorial for Reverend William McWhir, the principal of Sunbury Academy and a friend of General George Washington.

The 1854 Dorchester Church, which can be reached from Sunbury by a dirt road, is the only structure still intact from the mid-nineteenth century.

The Seabrook School is a new site nearby. Established in 1991, its exhibits include a restored one-room school and a living farm museum showcasing the traditions and crafts of rural African Americans around 1900. The site can be reached by traveling east on U.S. 84/GA 38.

Further Reading

"Fort Morris." *Georgia Magazine*. June-July 1968, pp. 21–23.

Georgia Writers' Project. *Drums and Shadows: Survival Studies among the Georgia Coastal Negroes*. Athens, GA: University of Georgia Press, 1986, pp. 112–119: "Sunbury."

Paul McIlvaine. *The Dead Towns of Sunbury, GA and Dorchester, SC*. Hendersonville, NC: Paul M. McIlvaine, 1971.

John McKay Sheftall. *Sunbury on the Medway: A Selective History of the Town, Inhabitants, and Fortifications*. State of Georgia, 1977.

DIRECTIONS

Fort Morris is seven miles east of I-95 (exit 13) off U.S. 84/GA 38. Open Tuesday-Saturday, 9 A.M.–5 P.M.; Sunday, 2 P.M.–5:30 P.M. Closed Thanksgiving and Christmas. Admission fee. Phone: (912) 884-5999. Living History demonstrations throughout the year reenact the history of Sunbury and incidents in the fort's history.

To reach the cemetery from the fort, turn right on Fort Morris Road at the entrance to Fort Morris Historic Site. Go one-half mile to Old Sunbury Road, then left one-tenth of a mile, and follow the signs to the cemetery.

$\mathcal{T}$HIRTEEN

Button Gwinnett's House

St. Catherines Island

Georgia was to be a "... happy flourishing colony ... free from the pest and scourge of mankind called lawyers."
— Provision for the new colony

$\mathcal{T}$he unspoiled island of St. Catherines, immediately south of Ossabaw Island, has a mixture few other sites can claim: shell rings of the Native American Creeks, remnants of a Spanish mission, slave cabins, a house associated with one of the signers of the Declaration of Independence, the country's first attempt at Black Separatism, and exotic animals. The island also has tidal marshes, which ocean-fed creeks fill and drain. Near the north end there is a sea bluff, a steep, twenty-foot bank overlooking the beach.

St. Catherines was once the capital of the Guale nation. These were the Native Americans who were living on the Georgia islands when European explorers first arrived in the sixteenth century. The Guales gave their name to this part of the coast, but disappeared from the area some three hundred years ago. The Guales may have chosen this island as their headquarters because of the high promontory on its east side, from which they could easily scan the ocean for intruders.

The name Guale (pronounced "Wally") was used for the island and for their chieftain, as well as for other Creek

tribes in the territory. The name may come from the Spanish pronunciation of the Indian word *wahali*, meaning "the south."

After Pedro Menendez founded St. Augustine in 1565 in what would become Florida, the Spanish sailed north along the coast. In 1566, on the island they called "Santa Catalina," the Spanish established a mission, from which missionaries spread out to other parts of the region. One of the Spanish missionaries at Santa Catalina, Domingo Augustin, wrote the first book in this country, a catechism and grammar in the Guale dialect for use in teaching them. That book has long since disappeared.

The sixteenth-century Spanish mission, Santa Catalina de Guale, was discovered in 1977, and is now the site of a major archaeological dig by New York's American Museum of Natural History.

The Jesuits, and then later the Franciscans, ran the mission. However, they finally abandoned it in 1680 after several bloody mutinies by the Native Americans and attacks from Charles Town by the English. The English arrived to settle Georgia in 1733, and General James Oglethorpe attempted to establish sites in the new colony. But when the Europeans returned to settle the islands in the eighteenth century, many of the Native Americans who still lived on the islands had to move elsewhere, partly to escape the European diseases that the foreigners brought to the island.

One amusing incident that took place on the island concerned the preacher, John Wesley. It occurred when he and the people he was traveling with from Frederica to Savannah were forced to take shelter on St. Catherines during a storm. One of the women on the boat was Miss Sophie Hopkey. This beautiful young woman, who was trying to win Wesley's heart, had hopes that the forced stay on the island, aided by a romantic campfire, might light an interest in the minister. No such luck — he spent the time discussing biblical verses to the discouraged Miss Sophie.

General Oglethorpe had agreed with Chief Tomochichi that the Creek tribes would retain control of several coastal islands. These would include Ossabaw, St. Catherines, and Sapelo, which the tribes would use for hunting and fishing. The Creeks soon had to give up the islands to the English, who moved there to farm and set up defensive forts.

One person who objected to the removal of the Creeks was an interpreter who had helped Oglethorpe with the local Native Americans: Mary Musgrove, a half-white, half-Creek woman who knew English (since she had been married to an English merchant) and who did much to soothe relations between the English and the Native Americans. The Creeks held Mary Musgrove in high regard, considering her to be a tribal princess. After she married Thomas Bosomworth, an English preacher to the settlers, both of them claimed that the Creeks had given her the three offshore islands, including St. Catherines.

When the Georgia Trustees objected to this claim, the Bosomworths took the case to court, where it dragged on for years. At one point in 1747, the Bosomworths, he in his canonical robes and she in her princess outfit, marched on Savannah with their Creek allies to press for their rights. Meanwhile, the Bosomworths cleared land on St. Catherines, built themselves a house, and began growing crops. The settlement of the case in 1760 gave the Bosomworths title to St. Catherines, but the governor was given the right to buy the other two islands from them.

Mary Bosomworth died soon after the 1760 decision, and Thomas remarried. He then sold the island to Button Gwinnett (1734–77), one of Georgia's three signers of the Declaration of Independence. Gwinnett came from England in 1765, became a merchant in Savannah, a member of the Commons House of Assembly in that city, and a justice for St. Johns Parish.

Gwinnett also helped write the state's first constitution, and he became the president of Georgia. He was killed in 1777 in a duel with General Lachlan McIntosh. Gwinnett and his wife had only one child, a daughter, who survived to maturity, but she apparently left no descendants. No reliable portraits of Button Gwinnett exist, and his very rare signature is purportedly worth $50,000.

Gwinnett may be buried in an unmarked grave on St. Catherines. It is near where visitors can still see what is called the "Old House," believed to have been the Gwinnetts' house. Gwinnett, so famous as a signer of one of the greatest documents in our country's history, was never financially successful and was unable to leave much money for his family when he died. The island soon reverted to the infamous Thomas Bosomworth, who returned there with his second wife. Bosomworth spent the rest of his life on the island, and is buried there with his family.

Immediately after the Civil War, during which time Union troops seized the abandoned islands, General Sherman established an independent state for freed slaves under the control of a man named Tunis Campbell. The "state" included the sea islands from Charleston, SC, to northern Florida, and its capital was at St. Catherines. The plan was short-lived, however, partly because developers, who were less than interested in letting the freedmen have such a beautiful island, bought up the best lots for themselves.

The island passed down to various buyers. Residents included the Rodriguez and Rauers families, who cultivated plantations on the island and established a huge private game preserve there. Another owner, Howard Coffin, who also owned nearby Sapelo Island, restored and enlarged Gwinnett's Old House. Nearby slave cabins, which were built around 1800, have been restored as guest houses.

In 1943, Edward Noble of New York bought the island for raising Black Angus cattle. Eleven years after Noble died in 1958, the island became part of the Edward J. Noble Foundation. The foundation allowed students in the University of Georgia's Forestry Department to do research there.

Today, St. Catherines is privately owned by the St. Catherines Island Foundation of New York. The foundation conducts research on both archeological sites and endangered animals. The American Museum of Natural History also does research on this National Historic Landmark site. The New York Zoological Society has stocked the island with rare and endangered species such as gazelles, zebra, antelopes, sandhill cranes, and the Abba Daba Tortoise, which prosper in the mild climate and lush vegetation. The animals are later shipped to large American zoos. At the present time, the island is not open to the public or to developers.

St. Catherines, along with Little Tybee, Williamson, Ossabaw, Blackbeard, Sapelo, Cabretta, Wolf, Little St. Simons, Little Cumberland, and Cumberland islands, is an undeveloped barrier island, especially compared to Tybee, St. Simons, Sea Island, and Jekyll Island. However, all of the islands have seen at least some alterations by people. Those alterations include the cutting down of forests and the growing of crops, such as sea-island cotton and sugar cane. But, unlike South Carolina to the north and Florida to the south, government officials have had some success in buying whole islands off the Georgia coast for preservation and wildlife refuges.

DIRECTIONS

St. Catherines is privately owned and not open to the public. Visitors can see it in the distance from Fort Morris.

Further Reading

Joan Anderson. *From Map to Museum: Uncovering Mysteries of the Past.* New York: Morrow Junior Books, 1988 [about an archeological dig on the island].

Margaret Davis Cate. "Saint Catherines Island." *Flags of Five Nations.* Sea Island, GA: Cloister Hotel, pp. 20–22.

Anthony Dees. "St. Catherine's Island: Georgia's Eden." *Georgia Journal*, March/April 1981, p. 9 and ff.

Betsy Fancher. *The Lost Legacy of Georgia's Golden Isles.* Garden City, NY: Doubleday, 1971, esp. pp. 121–142: "Tunis Campbell: Black Separatism on St. Catherine's Island."

David Hurst Thomas. *St. Catherines: An Island in Time.* Atlanta, GA: Georgia Humanities Council, 1988.

Burnette Vanstory. *Georgia's Land of the Golden Isles.* Athens, GA: University of Georgia Press, 1956, esp. pp. 22–27: "St. Catherine's Island."

 FOURTEEN

✍ Blackbeard the Pirate

Blackbeard Island

Only me and the Devil knows where that treasure is, and it'll go to the one who lives the longest.
  – Blackbeard the Pirate

Blackbeard Island, across Cabretta Inlet to the north of Sapelo, takes its name from the legendary pirate who preyed on ships up and down the seaboard in the early eighteenth century, about a decade before General Oglethorpe founded Georgia in 1733.

Blackbeard and other pirates attacked English and Spanish ships offshore and then sped away to hide in one of the many creeks, rivers, and inlets of coastal Georgia before officials could reach them. Today, the Refuge manager's house has a painting of Blackbeard hanging over the mantel, probably as a reminder of what might have transpired along the coast.

Born Edward Teach (or Thatch) in Bristol, England, in the late seventeenth century, Blackbeard at first served England as a privateer working out of Jamaica during the War of the Spanish Succession (1701–13). The end of that war put him and others like him out of the official privateering business and forced them to look for other means of supporting themselves.

In 1717, he and his band of cut-throats seized a French merchantman, changed its name to *Queen Anne's Revenge*, mounted forty guns on the ship, and began a reign of terror in the Caribbean and along the Florida and Georgia coasts. The coast of the southeastern United States was a perfect place to lie in wait for Spanish galleons on their way back to Spain after collecting silver and gold throughout the Caribbean.

Teach acquired his infamous nickname from his thick, black beard. He added to his notoriety by setting afire, just before attacking a ship, the pieces of cloth and tobacco he had put in his braided, dirty hair. The sight of the 6'4", 250-pound man, pistols in each hand, cutlass between his teeth, hair smoldering and producing thick, black smoke, probably gave him the psychological upper hand that enabled him to capture many ships.

His cruelty extended not only to the enemy, but also to his crew. At least once he extinguished the candles in his cabin and began shooting his pistols, wounding, maiming, even killing anyone in the way.

For several years (1716–18), he and his crew sailed from a North Carolina base, safe because of a pact with the governor there. A Royal Navy force sent from England in 1718 finally caught up with him and killed him. The Royal Navy crew decapitated him, placed his head on the top of the English ship as a deterrent to other pirates, and tossed his body overboard. That deed has inspired at least one ghost story in which the headless corpse of the pirate can be seen swimming in the area, looking for the rest of his body. Another tale swears there is a silver-plated cup made from Blackbeard's skull, complete with eye sockets on the lip of the cup.

Whether Blackbeard and other pirates ever buried treasure on this or any other Georgia island may never be known, but the possibility has spawned tales and rumors over the years. Unfortunately, pirates kept very few written records, least of all any on the locations of buried treasure. However, those who know the island well point to a large, rusted spike in one of the live oak trees, supposedly a pointer for returning pirates to find their hidden treasure. Legend has it that on this island Blackbeard behead-ed one of his wives, apparently his sixteenth, and six members of his crew, after which he buried them all in the sand, perhaps near here.

Blackbeard Island, like Wassaw, Ossabaw, and St. Catherines, is undeveloped, and measures 6.4 miles long and about two miles wide. Its interior has many parallel dune ridges, between which are low ridges that collect water during the wet season. The dunes represent earlier shorelines that have altered over time with changes in tidal movements and rising water levels.

The ownership of the island, which was for many years considered part of Sapelo Island, includes stories of the Creek tribe inhabiting the place, a French family owning it, and ownership claims by the Spanish. The United States Navy, which acquired the island in 1800 in a public auction, had hoped to cut the island's live oaks for building sturdy ships similar to the *Constitution*, the nineteenth-century frigate known as "Old Ironsides" because bullets could not penetrate her strong oak sides.

From 1880 to 1909, the National Board of Health used the island as a quarantine station for yellow fever victims, who were treated in a hospital at the south end of the island. A hurricane in 1898 destroyed that structure, but visitors can still see, on the north end, a brick crematory, built in 1904 and used for those who died of the disease.

In 1914, President Wilson made the island a wildlife preserve. In the following year, the federal government gave its jurisdiction to Georgia. In 1924, the U.S. Department of Agriculture took over the island, and permanently established it as a wildlife refuge. In 1940, a presidential proclamation made Blackbeard Island Reservation into Blackbeard Island National Wildlife Refuge administered by the U.S. Fish and Wildlife Service.

No firearms are allowed on the island, but hunters can take deer several times a year with bow and arrow. The proliferation of wild deer has led to controlled hunts, as well as the trapping and transporting of the animals to other sites.

Giant sea turtles use the isolated beaches of the island to lay their eggs, then return to the sea as they have done for thousands of years. The island is also home to numerous alligators.

The island has both freshwater and brackish ponds (the latter is a mixture of fresh and salt water). The ponds, some of which have been constructed by the Fish and Wildlife Service for the many birds that nest there, are the only real source of fresh water available to the animals on the island. Many oak, pine, and mixed hardwood trees flourish there.

About 17.5 nautical miles east of Blackbeard and Sapelo islands is Gray's Reef National Marine Sanctuary, also known as Sapelo Live Bottom. This is Georgia's only marine sanctuary. The purpose of the designation is to help prevent destruction of the reef and to regulate such activities as fishing and diving over the seventeen-square-mile area. The name of the reef honors Milton "Sam" Gray, a marine biologist who first discovered the rich flora and fauna there.

We may never know if Blackbeard used the island to hide himself or his loot in the early 1700s. If he did, he would have seen it much as it is now, a beautiful, isolated part of the Georgia coast.

The island, which is just to the north-northeast of Sapelo Island, can be reached by boat. Visitors can enjoy its beautiful beach, but must leave by dark.

Further Reading

Clinton V. Black. *Pirates of the West Indies*. Cambridge: Cambridge University Press, 1989, pp. 87–100.

Betsy Fancher. *The Lost Legacy of Georgia's Golden Isles*. Garden City, NY: Doubleday, 1971, esp. pp. 74–75.

Cyrus H. Karraker. *Piracy Was a Business*. Rindge, NH: Richard R. Smith, Publisher, 1953, pp. 140–164.

Robert E. Lee. *Blackbeard the Pirate: A Reappraisal of His Life and Times*. Winston-Salem, NC: John F. Blair, 1974.

Kevin M. McCarthy. *Twenty Florida Pirates*. Sarasota, FL: Pineapple Press, 1994, esp. pp. 46–49: "Blackbeard, 1718."

Ben Stahl. *Blackbeard's Ghost*. Boston: Houghton Mifflin, 1965.

Buddy Sullivan. *Early Days on the Georgia Tidewater: The Story of McIntosh County and Sapelo*. 4th edition. Darien, GA: McIntosh County Commission, 1995.

FIFTEEN

⌘ Sapelo Lighthouse

Sapelo Island

Over the centuries [Sapelo Island] has been many things: Aboriginal population center, prosperous cotton and sugar plantation, playground of the rich and famous, marine laboratory, and lately a state-owned wildlife preserve.

— Jerry Buckley and Larry Purdom, "Sapelo"

Sapelo Island, the fourth largest of the state's barrier islands, is also one of the highest, with parts of it reaching twenty feet above sea level. Four thousand years ago, humans lived, fished, and hunted on Sapelo. Over the years, the island has seen its share of missionaries, explorers, would-be developers, and environmentalists. Its name is adapted from that of the sixteenth-century Franciscan missionaries who built a convent there called San Jose de Zapala.

Today, visitors can take educational tours run by the Georgia Department of Natural Resources and marvel at the pristine beauty and abundance of wildlife on the island. Guides point out some of the hundreds of shell middens used by ancient Native Americans over four thousand years ago.

An early owner of the island, as well as of Ossabaw and St. Catherines islands, was Mary Musgrove, the part-Creek woman who married an Englishman, Thomas Bosomworth, and acted as interpreter for General Oglethorpe. The Creeks used Sapelo for hunting and fishing, but in 1757 ceded the island to England. Several owners controlled Sapelo

over the next decades, including some Frenchmen who had fled the French Revolution.

The man who did much to change Sapelo was Thomas Spalding, who owned it in the first half of the nineteenth century (1802–51). Besides harvesting its live oak trees, he grew sugar cane (the first planter in Georgia to do so), sea-island cotton, and rice. He also dug ditches to drain the marshy areas and make them more manageable. In 1809, Spalding built a sugar mill out of tabby, as well as a beautiful tabby house, the "South End House," which the Department of Natural Resources uses for conferences. As they tour the island by bus, visitors can see the tabby ruins of that sugar mill, whose grindstones were powered by animals.

Although Thomas Spalding's wife, Sarah, died in 1843, he continued to live on the island until his death in 1851. At that time, his son, Randolph Spalding, acquired the plantation, as well as his father's holdings on nearby Little Sapelo and Cabretta islands. The Spaldings continued to live on Sapelo Island until 1861, when Union troops landed there and forced the family to head for the mainland. The troops did so much damage that the house stood vacant until a Macon hunting club took it over around 1900. Cotton that the Spaldings had planted had by then succumbed to both the devastating boll weevil and the poor soil, which had been depleted after years of use.

Many freed slaves who had been taken inland during the Civil War by plantation owners fearful of the Union navy returned to the island after the war as free men and women. At that time, the Spaldings deeded to their former slaves a 434-acre, private part of the island known as "Hog Hammock." That plot of land, which the new freedmen had worked during slavery, was named after Sampson Hog, the man who took care of the Spaldings' hogs.

Some of the descendants of the Spalding slaves still live in the Hog Hammock community and are, in fact, the only private landowners on Sapelo. Their community center used to be a schoolhouse that the children had been taught in. Today, the residents' children are required to attend school on the mainland, which they reach by ferry each weekday.

Two churches on the island, St. Lukes Baptist Church and First African Baptist Church, share a minister and still attract many worshippers, some of them from the mainland.

Later owners of the island included Howard Coffin (owner from 1912 to 1934) and R.J. Reynolds of the Reynolds Tobacco Company (owner from 1934 until his death in 1964). Coffin, who helped establish Detroit's Hudson Motors and in 1928 opened Sea Island's Cloister Hotel, rebuilt the Spalding mansion and added some Mediterranean-style touches to his vacation retreat. There, he entertained such famous guests as President and Mrs. Calvin Coolidge and aviator Charles Lindbergh.

While his workers restored "South End House," Coffin's family lived in "Long Tabby," a temporary residence (1912-22) which later became a guesthouse. Much later, it was turned into a vacation retreat for underprivileged boys. One can visit the building, which has also served as a post office and the administrative center for the state's Department of Natural Resources.

Another interesting house that visitors can see is one of two identical structures that Howard Coffin built for two of his aunts. The women wanted to live on the island, but disliked each other too much to live in one house. Coffin had to build them separate, identical homes.

The island later became a hunting preserve for wealthy industrialists like Bernard Baruch, Isaac E. Emerson (the inventor of BromoSeltzer®), and Marshall Field. They liked to hunt the ducks that landed in the abandoned rice fields on their annual migrations along the seacoast.

On the bus tour of the island, visitors also see "Behavior Cemetery." Spalding opened this in the early 1800s and named it to encourage good conduct among his slaves. There is also an airstrip that Reynolds built on the open spaces of former cotton fields.

The lighthouse that stands on the southern shore of the island traces its origins to 1808, when the state of Georgia gave the federal government five acres of land that Thomas Spalding had once owned. But it wasn't until 1820 that Winslow Lewis of Boston constructed a ninety-foot-tall brick tower,

at the top of which was an iron lantern with sixteen-inch reflectors. He also built a keeper's house next door. The lighthouse guided mariners into the port of Darien, a prosperous site because of its location on the Altamaha River, and one that rivaled Savannah to the north.

In 1822, workers built a wooden range beacon at the northern tip of the Doboy Sound entrance. The beacon operated until 1899, but little remains today of the structure.

The lighthouse itself operated until Confederate troops dismantled it in 1862. After the Civil War, officials relit the tower for those vessels using the port at Darien. Workers painted the tower with red and white bands, an unusual color pattern.

By the 1890s, erosion and storms had damaged the structure so badly that in 1905 workers built a new, hundred-foot-tall steel tower, along with two cottages for the keepers.

A particularly dramatic incident occurred during the 1898 hurricane. As the lighthouse keeper was investigating the damage that had been done to the tower, he saw a wave wash his family out to sea. He had to swim out to rescue them.

The tower was finally dismantled in 1934, after a decrease in traffic for Darien made the tower unnecessary, and shipped to Grand Haven, Michigan. Visitors can still see the dilapidated old brick tower that Winslow Lewis built, but its light has long since been dimmed. However, Lewis's tower is now being restored by the State of Georgia and will be opened to the public in the near future.

Today, the island, which the Georgia Department of Natural Resources helps manage, comprises the R.J. Reynolds Wildlife Refuge for deer and wild turkey. The island's abundant wildlife includes not only deer and wild turkeys, but also endangered loggerhead turtles, which lay their eggs on the Sapelo beaches. The University of Georgia Marine Institute on the Sapelo Island National Estuarine Research Reserve conducts research on how best to preserve and protect these coastal islands.

DIRECTIONS

Visitors need to purchase ferry tickets to Sapelo Island at the Visitors' Center on Meridian Ferry dock. Guides accompany visitors on half-day bus tours around the island. Admission fee. To visit the island, visitors must be part of a guided tour, the guest of a resident, or an attendee at a conference. Phone: (912) 437-3224 or (912) 485-2251.

Further Reading

E. Merton Coulter. *Thomas Spalding of Sapelo*. Baton Rouge, LA: Louisiana State University Press, 1940.

Jerry Buckley and Larry Purdom. "Sapelo." *Georgia Journal*, May/June 1996, p. 12 and ff.

James Cerruti. "Sea Islands: Adventuring Along the South's Surprising Coast." *National Geographic*, March 1971, pp. 366–393.

Betsy Fancher. *The Lost Legacy of Georgia's Golden Isles*. Garden City, NY: Doubleday, 1971, esp. pp. 73–82: "Sapelo: A Journey Back in Time."

Georgia Writers' Project. *Drums and Shadows: Survival Studies among the Georgia Coastal Negroes*. Athens, GA: University of Georgia Press, 1986, pp. 158–172: "Sapelo Island."

Daniel P. Juengst, ed., *Sapelo Papers: Researches in the History and Prehistory of Sapelo Island, Georgia*. Carrollton, GA: West Georgia College, 1980.

William S. McFeely. *Sapelo's People*. New York: W.W. Norton, 1994.

Sara Pacher. "Sapelo's Seaside Feast." *Mother Earth News*, no. 119 (September/October 1989), pp. 80–83.

Buddy Sullivan. *Early Days on the Georgia Tidewater: The Story of McIntosh County and Sapelo*. 4th edition. Darien, GA: McIntosh County Commission, 1995.

Buddy Sullivan. "The Lighthouses of Georgia." *The Keeper's Log: The Quarterly Journal of the United States Lighthouse Society*, vol. 4, no. 3 (Spring 1988), pp. 2–11.

Buddy Sullivan. *Sapelo: A History*. Darien, GA: McIntosh County Chamber of Commerce, 1988.

$\mathscr{S}$IXTEEN

$\mathscr{S}$ Fort King George

Darien

Instead of green lawns, neat houses and plowed fields, around the fort were old Indian lands grown up into dense thickets, at the rear dark forests and in front only the wide river and vast expanse of marsh.
— Bessie Lewis, *They Called Their Town Darien*

$\mathscr{I}$n the early eighteenth century, the Georgia coast faced various potential invaders: the Native Americans and the French threatened from the west, and the Spanish from the south. The Georgia settlers asked England to build forts that would defend them and ensure their trade with interior towns. English authorities agreed on the need for forts and made plans to build Fort King George, named for England's King George I.

The fort stood at the mouth of the Altamaha River on Altamaha Bluff, where there had earlier been a Spanish mission and a Native American village. The fort thus became, during its short life (1721–32), the southern outpost of the British Empire in North America.

In 1721, John "Tuscarora Jack" Barnwell (so called because of his successful expedition against the Tuscarora tribe) came from Beaufort, South Carolina, bringing with him his Carolina Rangers. They began building Fort King George, a cypress blockhouse twenty-six feet square and forty feet high. The cypress sides of the blockhouse were four inches thick to protect those inside from musket shots. They also built thatched huts for barracks.

The fort was protected on two sides by a moat, in which there was a log palisade to deter attack from the land side. A branch of the Altamaha on another side provided further protection. That branch of the river, formerly called the "North Branch" of the Altamaha, is now known as "Lower Bluff Creek." Both the moat and the river were home to large alligators, which probably frightened the British soldiers as much as any enemy lurking nearby.

On the first floor of the blockhouse was a storage room for ammunition and supplies. The second floor was a gun room with two large windows from which soldiers could fire their large guns on enemy ships in the river. The floor also had smaller portholes for light artillery. The third floor was used as a lookout post. Near the blockhouse were palmetto-thatched huts, an officers' house, and a barracks for the ordinary soldiers.

The British soldiers stationed there were from His Majesty's 41st Independent Company, a group known as the "Invalid [IN-valid] Regiment," so called because so many of the soldiers were either sickly or victims of foreign campaigns.

For the next six years the soldiers stationed there came to hate the unhealthy site for its insects, disease, and weather. They had no fresh fruit or vegetables, and their meat rotted in the humid weather. Worst of all was the boredom of that isolated post.

By the end of the first year, most of the soldiers had died and were buried in the graves that can still be seen nearby. Each grave has a marker that says simply "Soldier of Fort King George." The cemetery has sixty-five grave sites, including seventeen for British soldiers who died in those early years. Visitors can see the site, one of the oldest British military cemeteries in the southeastern United States.

Those who survived were glad to leave there for good in 1727, after a fire destroyed most of the fort. Two lookouts remained on duty there, ready to warn settlers further north of invaders crossing the Altamaha.

Around 1735, when General Oglethorpe obtained land from the Creeks that extended south to the Altamaha River, he was determined to establish defenses along the new southern frontier. In January 1736, he brought in a group of 177 highland Scots from around Inverness, Scotland, to settle the area. They first moved into the fort and later to a new site, Fort Darien, which was on the Altamaha a mile upriver from Fort King George. The Scots settlers served Oglethorpe well, first when he attacked Spanish Florida in 1740 and then when the Spanish invaded Georgia in 1742 at the Battle of Bloody Marsh on St. Simons Island. One Native American, Tomochichi, sent six of his braves to the Scots to act as guides and hunters.

The new site, Darien, took its name from the settlement in Panama where Scots had unsuccessfully tried to establish themselves. Later, and only for a short time, the Georgia Scots changed the name of their new site to "New Inverness" to honor their homeland, but eventually the name of "Darien" was restored. The town on the Altamaha River became important for its sawmill industry, which provided considerable income to the area for many years.

Darien went on to become one of the nation's leading timber exporters because of its location on an important river. It also prospered from exporting cotton and rice. The timber business was interrupted in the 1860s during the Civil War, but resumed operations in the 1870s. Sawmilling in the area ended by 1925 after most of the large trees had been cut down.

When the sawmills closed, the site of Fort King George deteriorated. Weeds slowly obscured the place. Traces of the original fort had disappeared when the sawmills were built. Finally, local historians, among them Bessie Lewis, decided to reconstruct the fort, using maps from the British Colonial Record Office to find the exact site. In 1938, the state of Georgia bought the area as part of the state parks system and began to rebuild the fort.

Today, visitors can tour the replica of "Tuscarora Jack" Barnwell's original blockhouse as well as reconstructed earthworks and fort. Engineers reconstructed the forty-foot-high building in 1988. The fort, which is on the National Register of

Historic Places, is surrounded by wildlife, including marsh birds, snakes, even alligators.

In addition to the fort and a museum with artifacts and an audiovisual program, visitors can see the tabby ruins of a pre-Civil War house, the remains of a Spanish mission from the late 1500s, part of a village belonging to the Guale tribe in the 1600s, and a steam-powered circular sawmill and log basin from the early 1900s. There is also a nature trail through the nearby marsh.

On the way to Fort King George Historic Site, visitors can see St. Cyprian's Episcopal Church, built by ex-slaves in 1876. Named for a martyred African bishop, the church has been damaged by hurricanes, but is still in good shape.

❧

DIRECTIONS

The fort is located near Darien three miles east of I-95, exit 10, east on State Road 17. Fort King George is open 9 A.M.–5 P.M., Tuesday - Saturday; 2 P.M.–5:30 P.M., Sundays. Phone: (912) 437-4770. Closed Thanksgiving, Christmas Day, and New Year's Day. Admission fee. Special events during the year include Living History portrayals and enactments of different episodes in the history of the fort.

Further Reading

Joseph W. Barnwell. "Fort King George: Journal of Col. John Barnwell (Tuscarora) in the Construction of the Fort on the Altamaha in 1721." *The South Carolina Historical and Genealogical Magazine.* vol. 27, no. 4 (October 1926), pp. 189–203.

Jeannine Cook. *Fort King George: Step One to Statehood.* Valona, GA: no publ., 1990.

Ben W. Griffith, Jr. "Georgia's First English Settlement Now a Forgotten State Park." *The Atlanta Journal and Constitution Magazine.* October 9, 1960, p. 12 and ff.

Bessie Lewis. "Fort King George." *Georgia Magazine.* October–November 1967, pp. 22–24.

Bessie Lewis. *They Called Their Town Darien: Being a Short History of Darien and McIntosh County, Georgia.* Darien, GA: The Darien News, 1975.

John L. Nichols. "The Highland Independent Company of Foot and the Highland Rangers of Darien Georgia." *The Highlander,* November/December 1992, p. 65 and ff.

Buddy Sullivan. *Early Days on the Georgia Tidewater: The Story of McIntosh County & Sapelo.* 4th edition. Darien, GA: McIntosh County Commission, 1995.

$\mathcal{S}$EVENTEEN

$\mathcal{S}$ Butler Island Plantation

Butler Island

Scorn, derision, insult, menace—the handcuff, the lash—the tearing away of children from parents, of husbands from wives—the weary trudging in droves along the common highways, the labor of body, the despair of mind, the sickness of heart—these are the realities which belong to the system, and form the rule, rather than the exception, in the slave's experience."
— Fanny Kemble, *Journal of a Residence on a Georgian Plantation in 1838–1839*

$\mathcal{V}$isitors to beautiful Butler Island in the delta of the Altamaha River might be surprised to learn how the plantation that used to be there influenced the waning days of the Confederacy. It might, in fact, have helped end the Civil War.

The land south of the Altamaha developed slowly in the eighteenth century, partly because both South Carolina and Georgia claimed the land (a dispute later settled in Georgia's favor) and partly because planters liked the coastal islands better. The site of the Butler Island Plantation was excellent for rice cultivation because of its rich alluvial soil. Its nearness to the ocean took advantage of the daily tides, which forced the freshwater Altamaha River to flood or drain the fields. On the other hand, the distance of the plantation from the ocean prevented salt water from washing over the land and killing the crops.

Engineers from Holland installed dikes that reclaimed the fertile delta acres from the Altamaha River. Thus, in the nineteenth century, the 1,500-acre Butler Island just south of Darien became well known for having both orange groves and

one of the most successful rice plantations in the country.

In 1771, Irish-born Pierce Butler arrived in the American colonies as an officer in the British Army, and married Mary (Polly) Middleton, daughter of Thomas Middleton. Two years later, he resigned from the British Army and began a long career as a planter and politician. He represented his new home, South Carolina, in the Continental Congress, signed the Constitution, and became one of the first Carolinians elected to the U.S. Senate.

He also became friends with President George Washington and other statesmen. Among the many visitors to his island home was Aaron Burr, vice president of the United States and the man who killed Alexander Hamilton in a duel.

Butler's happy life ended in 1790, when his wife of nineteen years died. Some time after that, their son also died. The grief-stricken Butler left his home in Charleston, South Carolina, and bought land south of the Altamaha in Georgia. He developed the land into a profitable venture, partly due to the skill of his overseers.

Major Butler spent more of his time in Philadelphia, where he served as a director of the Bank of the United States and where he could visit with one of his daughters, Mrs. Sarah Butler Mease, and her family.

One of Mrs. Mease's sons, Pierce, was particularly close to his grandfather. When Butler died in 1822 at age 77, Pierce inherited his grandfather's coastal properties in Georgia. As part of the agreement that his grandfather had set down for any of his grandchildren who wanted to inherit the land, Pierce took his grandfather's last name, becoming Pierce Butler II. Years later, when young Pierce's brother John agreed to change his last name to Butler, Pierce gave him half of the Georgia property.

In 1834, Pierce Butler married the celebrated English actress, Frances (Fanny) Kemble, after she had completed a very successful tour of American cities. Originally, they settled in Philadelphia. Eventually Butler brought his wife and their two small daughters, Sarah and Frances, south to Georgia for a brief visit to his island home.

What Fanny saw on the island outraged her. Claiming to have had no previous knowledge that her husband was a slaveholder, the abolitionist Fanny was shocked at the many slaves her husband owned and the conditions under which they worked. At that time, the 280,000 slaves in Georgia represented over half the state's population. Many people believed slaves were necessary for the state's growing economy.

Fanny hoped she could free her husband's slaves—or at least alleviate their harsh living conditions. However, her efforts caused her relationship with her husband to deteriorate badly. She managed to live on the island with their children for just a few weeks in 1838–39 until she finally left in disgust. One of the items she took with her was the journal in which she had written about all that she had seen and experienced.

It was not long before the Butlers were divorced. The two daughters chose different sides: Sarah stayed with her mother, and Frances "Fanny" preferred to live with her father.

Later, when Fanny (the mother) was back in England, she learned that Confederate officials were applying for a loan from England to continue the Civil War. At first it seemed that the English, who were sympathetic to the South, would grant the loan. So Fanny published her diary, *Journal of a Residence on a Georgian Plantation in 1838–1839*. The book received wide circulation in England and was quoted in the British Parliament during a debate about the loan. It galvanized British public opinion against the South, much as Harriet Beecher Stowe's book, *Uncle Tom's Cabin*, had done in America's North. Parliament refused to make the loan, and the war was thus shortened to some degree.

After the Civil War, Pierce Butler and his daughter Fanny moved back to their plantation, but found it difficult to manage in those days of Reconstruction, without the help of slaves. Fanny later wrote her own book, *Ten Years on a Georgia Plantation Since the War*, in which she tried to refute her mother's views about the plantation by describing life there during Reconstruction.

After Pierce died in 1867, Fanny remained

on the island until she married the Rt. Rev. J.W. Leigh. One of their visitors to the island in those years was her sister Sarah's husband, novelist Owen Wister, author of the highly successful novel, *The Virginian*.

In 1925, Colonel T.L. Huston bought the island and raised one of the most successful Guernsey herds in the Southeast. He was also able to grow large crops of iceberg lettuce, after he rebuilt the old dikes on what continued to be called the Butler Island Plantation.

Because Huston was a part-owner of the New York Yankees in the 1920s, many baseball players, including Babe Ruth, visited the island.

Today, the slave cabins, the houses of the overseers, and the old overseers' house where the Kembles had lived are all gone. However, visitors can still see the beautiful two-storied white clapboard house built by Colonel Huston in 1927 (shown here). Also clearly visible is a 75-foot-tall brick chimney that used to be part of a steam-powered rice mill built by slaves in the 1850s.

Those who are interested may wish to read *The Waiting Time*, a novel by the late Eugenia Price about a woman who resembles Fanny Kemble.

In 1954, Butler Island became part of the Butler Island Waterfowl Management Area, the first state wildfowl refuge in Georgia. The Georgia State Game and Fish Department bought Butler Island, along with the islands of Champneys, Rhetts, Broughton, and Cambers, to preserve them as wildlife refuges. Scientists realized that the vacant rice fields on the islands would attract thousands of ducks and geese on their annual migration along the Atlantic Flyway.

DIRECTIONS

Butler Island is off U.S. 17 just south of Darien.

Further Reading

Margaret Armstrong. *Fanny Kemble: A Passionate Victorian*. New York: Macmillan Co., 1938.

Malcolm Bell, Jr. *Major Butler's Legacy: Five Generations of a Slaveholding Family*. Athens, GA: University of Georgia Press, 1987.

Margaret Davis Cate. *Early Days of Coastal Georgia*. St. Simons Island, GA: Fort Frederica Association, 1955, esp. pp. 116–23.

Betsy Fancher. *The Lost Legacy of Georgia's Golden Isles*. Garden City, NY: Doubleday, 1971, esp. pp. 101–19: "Fanny Kemble: An Actress Looks at Slavery."

Don W. Farrant. *The Lure and Lore of the Golden Isles: The Magical Heritage of Georgia's Outerbanks*. Nashville, TN: Rutledge Hill Press, 1993, esp. pp. 37–41: "Liverpool Hazzard" [about a former slave of Pierce Butler].

Fanny Kemble. *Journal of a Residence on a Georgian Plantation in 1838–1839*. New York: Knopf, 1961.

Frances Butler Leigh. *Ten Years on a Georgia Plantation Since the War*. New York: Negro Universities Press, 1969.

Eugenia Price. *The Waiting Time*. Garden City, NY: Doubleday, 1997.

Buddy Sullivan. *Early Days on the Georgia Tidewater: The Story of McIntosh County and Sapelo*. 4th edition. Darien, GA: McIntosh County Commission, 1995.

Burnette Vanstory. *Georgia's Land of the Golden Isles*. Athens, GA: University of Georgia Press, 1956, esp. pp. 84–90 [about Butler Island].

Constance Wright. *Fanny Kemble and the Lovely Land*. New York: Dodd, Mead & Company, 1972.

EIGHTEEN

❧ Hofwyl-Broadfield Plantation

north of Brunswick

Long days beneath the torrid Dixie sun
In miasma'd rice swamps
— Sterling Brown

The Altamaha River in south Georgia has played a significant role in nearly every facet of the state's history. It affected the geologic history because by carrying large amounts of sediment to the sea, it helped form Little St. Simons Island to the east. It influenced the religious history, as Spanish missionaries established missions in the seventeenth century along the river to convert the Native Americans. Militarily, the river was the site of Fort King George, the first fort to challenge the Spanish and French for the area. The Altamaha also served for a long time as the boundary between the English and Spanish dominions in North America. And it profoundly affected Georgia's agriculture, since the area was perfect for the cultivation of rice.

Just how important rice was to the economy of Georgia and how the Altamaha River contributed to that cultivation becomes apparent when visiting the Hofwyl-Broadfield Plantation, a state historic site between Darien and Brunswick. There, visitors can see an antebellum home that dates back to 1851 and whose furnishings date from the

eighteenth and nineteenth centuries. The site includes a rice plantation, a museum with a movie about planters and slaves, and exhibits that show what life used to be like on such farms. Because so many other plantations from the eighteenth century have been destroyed, Hofwyl-Broadfield, in a sense, represents all such places.

The nearby Altamaha River was the southern boundary of Georgia until 1763. In that year, the treaty that ended the French and Indian War between England and France extended Georgia's southern boundary to the St. Marys River, the northern border of Florida. This new extension allowed farmers from Georgia and South Carolina to plant rice south of the Altamaha, but they needed hundreds of slaves to do the back-breaking work.

Many of those slaves were from western Africa, where they had learned to cultivate rice. Their knowledge of farming methods helped the Georgian slaveowners to increase the productivity of the plantations. For example, the slaves used canals along the Altamaha for irrigation purposes: The location of this and other plantations was conducive to rice growing because the low-lying fields were three miles above the ocean and near fresh-water rivers. The proximity to the ocean allowed the tides to flood the fields with fresh water and then drain them, and the three-mile distance from the ocean prevented the salt water from reaching the rice fields and killing them. The floodgates that the slaves built controlled the tidal flow of the necessary fresh water to the fields. Such skillful use of the river enabled the plantation owners to produce a crop that they sent to many parts of the world.

This particular plantation represents just one of the twenty or more rice plantations that once flourished in the area. Between 1850 and 1860, the plantations along the Altamaha produced more than 100,000 pounds of rice annually, a truly staggering figure that explains how important such plantations were to the Georgian economy. Although plantation owners along the Altamaha prospered, they, like other farmers, had to cope with the vagaries of weather, tide, insects, and the price fluctuations of the rice market.

Hofwyl-Broadfield, which is on the mainland west of Little St. Simons Island, traces its origins to William Brailsford of Charleston. In 1807, Brailsford started cultivating rice along the Altamaha. The work was continued by his son-in-law, James Troup, who eventually owned 357 slaves, over seven thousand acres, and several homes.

The Broadfield Plantation, as it was known in the first half of the nineteenth century, added the name Hofwyl (pronounced "hah-fill") after one of its owners, George Dent, built a house there in 1851. Dent, who called the house "Hofwyl" after a school he had attended in Switzerland, had married Ophelia, daughter of James Troup.

At Hofwyl-Broadfield, visitors can walk along the well-marked trails and see just what life must have been like there two hundred years ago. Displays explain how slaves built the canals for irrigation and transportation, how dikes were used for the cultivation of rice, and how workers built up the land that they would use when the fields were flooded by the river.

There still exists on the grounds the shed from which wages were paid to the former slaves who remained on the plantation after the Civil War. When the slaves were freed, many of them settled in nearby towns and continued to work at the same jobs they had done as slaves, but now they were paid for their labor as free men.

The names of some of the new communities told their own stories. Petersville honored an ex-slave named Peter. Needwood came from the fact that the ex-slaves there needed wood to keep their cooking fires going. Freedman's Rest is self-explanatory.

Besides the slaves, those plantations required skilled laborers: managers to operate the mills; carpenters and mechanics to keep the machinery running well; coopers to make barrels; brick masons to build structures; and other skilled workers to keep the plantation running smoothly.

Signs also explain that one of the twentieth-century owners, James Dent, the son of George and Ophelia Dent, concluded that mosquitoes were the cause of the malaria that killed many Georgians

during the hot, humid summers. Others thought malaria was caused by miasmas or "bad air" from the swamp. Unlike other planters who escaped for the summer months to the mountains, Dent stayed home—but he had screens installed on his windows and doors. The screens kept the mosquitoes out of the house, helped prevent malaria among his family members, and convinced other planters to do the same.

The plantation produced a steady supply of rice until the Civil War. During the early 1860s, the white men of the family went off to serve in the Confederacy, the slaves were freed, and the buildings deteriorated from the weather and lack of maintenance. In the second half of the nineteenth century, family members tried to revive the growing of rice. When that venture failed, they grew cotton, corn, and grain.

In the first years of the twentieth century, a shortage of labor and several strong hurricanes destroyed the rice fields. Rather than rebuild, the owners of the plantation converted it into a dairy. Among the many local people who bought the dairy's milk were the millionaires who spent the winter months on nearby Jekyll Island.

The same family owned the plantation from 1804 until 1973, prospering through efficient farming and milk-producing methods. The dairy produced milk for Glynn County until 1942, when it finally closed. In 1973, the state of Georgia acquired the site and later opened it to the public, making available a special part of the state's history.

DIRECTIONS

The plantation is located at 5556 U.S. Highway 17N, about fifteen miles north of Brunswick and south of Darien. Take exit 9 of I-95 and head north on State Road 99. Open year-round, Tuesday-Saturday, 9 A.M.–5 P.M. Sunday, 2 P.M.–5:30 P.M. Closed Mondays and Tuesdays after legal holidays; Thanksgiving, Christmas Day, and New Year's Day. Admission fee. Phone: (912) 264-9263.

Further Reading

Charles Joyner. *Remember Me: Slave Life in Coastal Georgia.* Atlanta, GA: Georgia Humanities Council, 1989.

Julia Floyd Smith. *Slavery and Rice Culture in Low Country Georgia, 1750–1860.* Knoxville, TN: University of Tennessee Press, 1985.

Buddy Sullivan. *Early Days on the Georgia Tidewater: The Story of McIntosh County and Sapelo.* 4th edition. Darien, GA: McIntosh County Commission, 1995.

NINETEEN

↬ Liberty Ships

Brunswick

The mission of this ship was not glamorous, her task seldom dangerous; no headlines were captured for the folks back home; nobody on board became a hero, unless doing a job with a minimum of complaining and soldiering and a maximum of loyalness, cheerfulness and diligence can be said to make a man a hero.

— John Bunker, *Liberty Ships*

The significance of Brunswick as a place where Liberty Ships were built relates to how much the town suffered in the name of liberty, and how much it depended on the sea for its livelihood, whether with shrimping, fishing, boating, or shipbuilding.

The site on which modern Brunswick stands was first known as "Carr's Fields," after an early settler. Captain Mark Carr arrived in Georgia in 1738 and established a corn and tobacco plantation at a place called Plug Point. The name was changed to Brunswick in 1771 to honor the British royal family, who were descended from the House of Brunswick. Town planners named some of the squares and streets with the very English names of Gloucester, London, Newcastle, and Prince. The pro-English sentiment of the people in Brunswick changed during the Revolutionary War when many (though not all) Georgians supported American independence.

Brunswick is the county seat of Glynn, one of the eight original counties organized in 1777 under Georgia's constitution. The name honored John Glynn, a member of the British House of Commons who supported American independence.

As the town prospered in the eighteenth and early nineteenth centuries, its citizens wanted to see just how good their local products were. For example, they wondered if their locally made boats could compete with those made elsewhere. So in 1837 they went to New York and challenged boaters there to compete in a race.

When the New Yorkers didn't accept the challenge, the people of Brunswick challenged a boating club at Augusta to a race on the Savannah River. Why Augusta? The boating club there had bought some New York-made boats that had successfully competed in Hudson River races. So, if the Brunswickers could not get New York boaters to compete, maybe they could get New York-made boats to race.

But it was not to be. The Augusta club refused to take up the challenge. Undaunted, the local people finally staged a race in January 1838, but only local boats competed. The thousands of people who showed up could only wonder if the Brunswick boats could have beaten the New Yorkers on the river.

During the Civil War, because Brunswick was a port and therefore vulnerable to enemy attack or blockade, many citizens abandoned the town, and federal troops moved in.

After the war, the town suffered a yellow fever outbreak in 1876, and business once again declined, but the town and county recovered in the 1880s as the timber industry prospered.

By the 1890s, Brunswick stood second in the world's leading exporters of naval stores (Savannah was first).

The opening of the causeway to St. Simons Island in 1924 brought many visitors to the area. Sidney Lanier made the nearby salt marshes famous with his poem, "Marshes of Glynn," and prosperity seemed close at hand. Then came the Second World War.

World War II affected the town in several ways. Coastal shipping was threatened by German U-boats, which were sinking unescorted merchant vessels almost at will. For example, on April 8, 1942, a German U-boat sank two tankers off the coast of St. Simons Island: S.S. *Oklahoma* and S.S. *Esso Baton Rouge*. To neutralize the U-boats, the federal government built the Glynco Naval Air Station, the "Blimp Base," six miles north of Brunswick.

Why Brunswick? Two reasons: first, because the town was near the sea over which the blimps would fly, looking for submarines; and second, because the area had no tall structures that could interfere with the blimps.

However, there was one major problem with constructing such a large facility. Two hangars had to be built that could accommodate six blimps at the same time, and there was almost no steel to be had during the war. Therefore, engineers had to use wood to build the hangars, which turned out to be the largest such structures in the world at that time. The workers did such a good job that the hangars stood until 1964, when Hurricane Dora damaged them. Later, they were torn down.

The blimps patrolled the offshore waters and protected the convoys of ships that sailed up and down the east coast. By the end of the war, the blimps from Brunswick had escorted 98,000 ships without losing any to the U-boats.

The site is now used for the Federal Law Enforcement Training Center.

The other World War II-related activity in Brunswick was the construction of Liberty Ships, the mass-produced freighters that became so important for shipping large amounts of cargo during the war. In 1942, after the loss of more than five hundred million tons of vessels and cargo to German submarines, the U.S. Maritime Commission picked sixteen sites around the country to build the huge, strong cargo ships that became known as Liberty Ships. Brunswick was one of those sites.

Because their design was very basic, these workhorse ships were quickly and easily built. The vessels were over four hundred feet long, could carry up to ten thousand tons, and traveled at a top speed of about sixteen miles per hour.

The Maritime Commission officially designated the ships EC2: "E" for Emergency, "C" for Cargo, and "2" for large capacity. The U.S. Army and Navy adapted them for many uses, including hospital ships, repair vessels, troop transports, and picket duty.

The J.A. Jones Construction Company of Charlotte, North Carolina, was in charge of building the Brunswick Liberty Ships. The company hired sixteen thousand local workers to work in local shipyards, and the weekly payroll of one million dollars greatly helped Brunswick's economy. More importantly, the people knew they were aiding the war effort in a major way.

The shipyards in Brunswick produced about four Liberty Ships a month; by the end of World War II, the workers had built ninety-nine Liberty Ships. Typical of the spirit of the Brunswick workers was the fact that the workers worked on Christmas Day in 1944, and refused to take any overtime pay for their extra work.

Although the ships had official names like U.S.S. *Coastal Ranger*, *Crown & Diamond*, and *Shell Bar*, their names were painted over and they sailed the Atlantic and Pacific anonymously. This disguised their origin and cargo from the enemy.

After World War II and the closing of the local shipyards, Brunswick displayed for twenty years a cut-away scale model of a Liberty Ship. The model finally deteriorated so badly that it had to be removed from the foot of the Torras Causeway leading to St. Simons Island. In 1991, the city replaced it with another scale model, a twenty-three-foot-long vessel that they named *City of Brunswick*.

The ships built in the Brunswick shipyards continued to serve their country long after World War II. Some were transferred to Russia as part of the Lend-Lease Program. Others sailed the seas under many different flags, names, and purposes. The Navy's last Liberty Ship was finally decommissioned in 1972. Thus ended the long service of the almost three thousand Liberty Ships.

DIRECTIONS

Visitors can see the scale model of the Liberty Ship on U.S. 17 at the Welcome Center near the entrance to the Torras Causeway leading to St. Simons Island.

Further Reading

John Gorley Bunker. *Liberty Ships: The Ugly Ducklings of World War II*. Annapolis, MD: Naval Institute Press, 1972.

"German U-Boat attack off St. Simons recalled." *The Brunswick News*, December 7, 1996, p. 5A.

Nancy Rhyne. *Touring the Coastal Georgia Backroads*. Winston-Salem, NC: John F. Blair Publisher, 1994.

TWENTY

Christ Church

St. Simons Island

It was not any apprehension of my own danger (though my life had been threatened many times) but an utter despair of doing good there [at Fort Frederica], which made me content with the thought of seeing it no more.
— John Wesley, founder of Methodism

The name of St. Simons comes from the main mission, which the Spanish called "San Simon." Franciscan missionaries followed the Jesuits, but had no better luck than the Jesuits in converting the indigenous peoples. The first inhabitants of St. Simons were the Guale tribe, whose name for the island was "Asao." The Guales were followed in the seventeenth century by Spanish Jesuit missionaries from St. Augustine, Florida, who tried (not very successfully) to convert the Indians to Christianity.

Thus, the religious history of St. Simons must include the three missions that the Spanish established on what they called "Isla de Asao." It should also include the "German Village" (sometimes called "The Village" today) that a number of Lutherans from Salzburg, Austria, founded in their search for freedom of worship. And such a history would have to make particular mention of Christ Church, one of the island's prettiest buildings.

The history of Christ Church draws from a double heritage: Near it is a place where religious leaders and laypeople

still meet today. This is the beautiful Methodist Conference Center, Epworth-by-the-Sea, which was built in 1952 as a memorial to the two great Methodist leaders from England: John (1703–91) and Charles Wesley (1707–88).

In 1735, the Wesleys accompanied General James Oglethorpe to the new colony of Georgia, where they had hoped to minister to the religious needs of the settlers and possibly convert the Native Americans to Christianity. An organization in England, The Society for Propagating the Gospel in Foreign Parts, paid the Wesleys' salaries and had high hopes for them.

When John Wesley arrived in Georgia, he began working as a chaplain at Fort Frederica on St. Simons. But his beliefs were such that he angered the wife of the fort's doctor, and when he called into question the sincerity of her religious conversion, she threatened to shoot him. By 1737, when his efforts to proselytize angered many settlers in the Georgia colony, he returned to England, where his hard work and efforts paid off in the founding of Methodism.

Charles Wesley, Oglethorpe's secretary and the official "Secretary for Indian Affairs," also became discouraged with Georgia. He returned to England in 1736. There he became the country's greatest hymn writer, composing such classics as "Hark, the Herald Angels Sing" and "Love Divine, All Loves Excelling."

The legacy of the two Wesley brothers is evident today in the beautiful Christ Church. The building, with its tall belfry and narrow stained-glass windows, is set amid trees draped with Spanish moss. However, while Christ Church traces its origins to the day when General Oglethorpe gathered his newly landed troops for evening prayer, the actual structure dates from the nineteenth century.

The parish of Christ Church, which was originally organized in 1807, is the second oldest Episcopal Church in the Diocese of Georgia. Before its members had a church to congregate in, they met in their individual homes. For the church site, officials chose land near Fort Frederica, where John and Charles Wesley had preached to the soldiers in 1736.

The first rector of the parish was Reverend William Bests of Savannah.

Economic hardships brought on by the War of 1812, such as embargoes and other restrictions, delayed the construction of the first Christ Church building until 1820. Three years later, the congregation joined with Christ Church, Savannah, and St. Paul's Church, Augusta, to form the Diocese of Georgia.

At one point, when church officers wondered where they would obtain the money needed to repair the building and construct a vestry room, they discovered a large amount of honey in a beehive in the belfry. From then on, many referred to the place as the "Bee Hive Church."

The first small church building lasted until Union troops in the Civil War damaged it so badly that members once again had to hold services in their homes.

In the 1870s, Anson Green Phelps Dodge, Jr. moved to the island to help harvest lumber. When he saw how badly Christ Church was deteriorating, he decided to replace it with a new building. He dedicated the new church to his first wife, Ellen, who had died on their honeymoon in India. Dodge eventually left the lumber business and became a minister. He established the Dodge Home for Boys, and became rector of Christ Church in 1884, serving there until he died in 1898.

A stained-glass window in the white-frame, Gothic-style church depicts him with the son from his second marriage, a boy who was tragically killed after falling from a horse.

The old churchyard nearby has gravestones belonging to many important people in the history of St. Simons Island: Ann Armstrong, whose gravesite has a sago palm, supposedly brought the tree from the Bahamas and successfully introduced it to the local plantations; John Couper, who planted olives and dates on the island; Reverend Anson Dodge, who ministered to the congregation for many years, and his family; Thomas Butler King of Retreat Plantation, who served in the House of Representatives for more than a decade; and Lucien Knight, who was the first state historian of Georgia.

John Wylly, whose tombstone notes that he "fell a victim to his generous courage," was killed in 1838 by a neighbor, Dr. Thomas Hazzard, over a property-line dispute.

One gravesite in particular should be mentioned, that of Captain Lord King. One of the King family's slaves, Neptune Small, accompanied Lord King, whom Neptune had served for many years, when the King boys went off to fight for the Confederacy in the Civil War. When Lord King was killed in the Battle of Fredericksburg in 1862, Neptune carried Lord's body off the field and transported it back hundreds of miles, over rivers and through marshes, so that it could be interred in the King family plot at Christ Church Cemetery. Neptune then returned to Virginia to be with another of the King boys until the end of the war. Neptune Park near the pier on St. Simons honors that loyal man.

Local novelist Eugenia Price, who is also buried in Christ Church Cemetery, profiled the church in her novels about St. Simons: *Lighthouse*, which is about living on the island and building the lighthouse [1787–1820]; *Bright Captivity*, about John Couper's Cannon's Point Plantation [1803–1817] and *Where Shadows Go*, about other plantations there [1825–1839]; *New Moon Rising*, on the pre-Civil War period [1830–1865], and *Beauty From Ashes*, about a later period [1845–1864]; and *The Beloved Invader*, about Reconstruction [1879–1898]. Her *St. Simons Memoir* and *At Home on St. Simons* describe her life on the island and how she came to write her popular novels.

DIRECTIONS

Christ Church is on St. Simons Island, twelve miles from the mainland. It is reached by causeway and toll road from Brunswick. When you go onto the island, turn left onto Sea Island Road and then left onto Frederica Road. Follow the signs to the church and cemetery.

Further Reading

Margaret Davis Cate. *Early Days of Coastal Georgia*. St. Simons Island, GA: Fort Frederica Association, 1955, esp. pp. 40–49.

Betsy Fancher. *The Lost Legacy of Georgia's Golden Isles*. Garden City, NY: Doubleday, 1971, esp. pp. 148–156.

Don W. Farrant. *The Lure and Lore of the Golden Isles*. Nashville, TN: Rutledge Hill Press, 1993, esp. pp. 30-33, 74–75.

Eugenia Price. *At Home on St. Simons*. Atlanta, GA: Peachtree Publishers, 1981.

Eugenia Price. *Beauty From Ashes*. New York: Doubleday, 1995.

Eugenia Price. *The Beloved Invader*. 1965; Nashville, TN: Rutledge Hill Press, 1985.

Eugenia Price. *Bright Captivity*. New York: Doubleday, 1991.

Eugenia Price. *Lighthouse*. 1971; Nashville, TN: Rutledge Hill Press, 1985.

Eugenia Price. *New Moon Rising*. 1969; Nashville, TN: Rutledge Hill Press, 1985.

Eugenia Price. *St. Simons Memoir*. Philadelphia, PA: Lippincott, 1978.

Eugenia Price. *Where Shadows Go*. New York: Doubleday, 1993.

Burnette Vanstory. *Georgia's Land of the Golden Isles*. Athens, GA: University of Georgia Press, 1956, esp. pp. 125–129: "Christ Church, Frederica."

Mary Bray Wheeler. *Eugenia Price's South: A Guide to the People and Places of Her Beloved Region*. Atlanta, GA: Longstreet Press, 1993.

$\mathscr{T}$WENTY-ONE

✌ Fort Frederica

St. Simons Island

Frederica will always hold an honoured place in American history as the bastion upon which the security of Georgia and the southern colonies depended.
— Trevor R. Reese, *Frederica*

$\mathscr{I}$n the early eighteenth century, southern Georgia, especially the strategic coastal islands, was coveted by three European powers: Spain, France, and England. Spain controlled Florida and was considering reestablishing the Georgia missions it had abandoned. France had established settlements at the mouth of the Alabama River to the west of Georgia, and wanted to extend to the east. England had established its colonies north of Georgia, but wanted to expand down to the Florida border.

In 1736, three years after he founded Savannah, General James Edward Oglethorpe saw the need to protect the newest English colony on the east coast of the United States. He therefore had his soldiers build a fort on the west side of St. Simons Island. He called it "Fort Frederica," and named the surrounding thirty-five-acre walled town "Frederica" in honor of Frederick Louis, Prince of Wales, and the eldest son of Georgia's namesake, King George II. (Frederick Louis died before he could become King of England, but his son became King George III.)

Some called the new fort the "Gibraltar of North

86

America" because of its importance in defending the English colonies from the Spanish and French. Oglethorpe himself preferred the new settlement over Savannah. He built at Frederica the only house he ever owned in the colonies, and lived there for ten years. We can still see today remains of Oglethorpe's home and the houses of the town, which were made of tabby, the local mixture of sand, lime, oyster shell, and water that made a very hard building material. The workers obtained the lime by burning oyster shells they gathered from ancient Native American shell mounds.

The town, which began with forty-four men and seventy-two women and children, eventually reached a population of approximately a thousand residents. They made the settlement self-sufficient with the crops they raised. The combination of careful planning by Oglethorpe, assistance from friendly Guales, and hard work by the settlers got the town off to a successful start.

In the late 1730s, England and Spain threatened each other in what came to be called the "War of Jenkins' Ear" (1739-48), so called after an incident during which Spanish soldiers captured the English ship *Rebecca*, and cut off the ear of a British sailor named Jenkins. This was all the provocation the English needed to attack Spain's fort in St. Augustine.

Although the English troops sacked the little Florida town, they could not capture or enter the impregnable Castillo de San Marcos, so they returned to Georgia, knowing full well that the Spanish would retaliate. This is exactly what happened. In 1742, Spanish troops landed on St. Simons and prepared to attack Fort Frederica. Oglethorpe's forces were lying in wait and ambushed the Spanish soldiers, who were marching single file down a narrow trail. The English forces captured or killed most of the 170 Spanish and Native Americans. When the Spanish returned with new troops, Oglethorpe's soldiers, especially his Highlanders, captured or killed around two hundred of them. The action took place near an open marsh on St. Simons in what came to be known as the "Battle of Bloody Marsh." Decisively defeated, the Spanish withdrew to Florida

and never again threatened Georgia or the other English colonies.

Once it became clear that the Spanish would not invade Georgia again, the English troops at Frederica withdrew. By 1749, the town had been abandoned. The residents, who were mostly artisans and tradesmen who depended on the military for protection, went elsewhere for work, and the town began to disintegrate.

In the 1770s, James Spalding, a farmer who had supported England in the days before American independence, began farming a large plantation on St. Simons, but left the island during the Revolutionary War. He later returned to find his home and plantation in ruins, but decided to settle there anyway and grow sea-island cotton, a crop that could only survive on the South Carolina and Georgia islands. So successful were the Spaldings and other plantation owners in growing and selling sea-island cotton that by the early 1800s, they had all built expensive, elegant homes on St. Simons.

During the Revolutionary War and the War of 1812, workers went to St. Simons to cut down its live oaks. The timber was excellent for building warships, including the U.S.S. *Constitution*, "Old Ironsides," which is still commissioned.

Although English troops destroyed some island homes during the War of 1812, the planters later rebuilt them. The Civil War was more devastating, but in the 1870s, some of the planters managed to prosper by running profitable sawmills. Early in this century, many tourists discovered the beaches of St. Simons and flocked to the little island. Steamships transported the visitors until a causeway opened in 1924, making the island more accessible.

Those who were interested in preserving the fort established the Fort Frederica Association and bought seventy-eight acres of the site. In 1945, they donated the land to the United States for a national monument. After two centuries of deterioration and neglect, the site began to be restored. However, the fort itself was long gone.

Although we can see little today of the fort or the town, a museum there has a film about the place, exhibits showing the different time periods, and well-marked paths visitors can use to walk the grounds. The remains of the fort and the tabby powder magazine near the Frederica River are still visible. Signs throughout the grounds indicate what each building was used for. The National Park Service administers Fort Frederica National Monument.

DIRECTIONS

The fort is further down the road from Christ Church. Hours: 8 A.M.–5 P.M. daily except Christmas; summer hours may be extended. Inquire about Living History demonstrations during the summer. Admission fee. Phone: (912) 638-3639. Visitors can also visit the site of the Battle of Bloody Marsh, which is off Demere Road east of Frederica Road.

Further Reading

Tommy E. Jenkins. *A Graphic History of St. Simons Island.* St. Simons Island, GA: Tommy E. Jenkins, 1994, esp. pp. 14–33.

Francis Moore. "A Voyage to Georgia, 1744," Re-published by Fort Frederica Association, 1992.

Trevor R. Reese. *Frederica: Colonial Fort and Town: Its Place in History.* St. Simons Island, GA: Fort Frederica Association, 1969.

Willy Folk St. John. "Digging Up the Past at Frederica." *Atlanta Journal Magazine,* August 4, 1946, pp. 8–9.

∿ St. Simons Lighthouse

St. Simons Island

The tall, white St. Simons lighthouse has long been haunted by unexplainable footsteps going up and down the spiral stairway.
— Burnette Vanstory, *Ghost Stories & Superstitions of Old Saint Simons*

$\mathcal{T}$his imposing tower rises at the southern end of St. Simons Island. It serves the port of Brunswick to the west on the mainland, and is one of only five active lighthouses in Georgia today. It is also one of this nation's oldest continuously working lighthouses. It protects the southern tip of this, one of Georgia's largest and most developed barrier islands.

In 1736, General James Oglethorpe built Fort St. Simons to protect the settlers from attack by Spanish troops stationed in Florida. When the English successfully warded off the Spanish at the Battle of Bloody Marsh, settlers moved into the area to take advantage of the rich soil and good offshore fishing.

In the early 1800s, John Couper, a plantation owner on St. Simons, bought the site of the fort, renamed it "Couper's Point," and then in 1804 sold the land to the government for one dollar. His plan was for federal officials to build a lighthouse at the entrance to St. Simons Sound.

In 1807, the U.S. Lighthouse Service contracted with James Gould, newly arrived from New England and in search

of work, to build a seventy-five-foot tall lighthouse at Couper's Point. It took Gould three years to finish the octagonal tower. Its base was twenty-five feet in diameter, tapering to ten feet at the top. The cost of the completed tower was only $13,775. Gould needed strong material for the construction. He used tabby, a concrete-like mixture of lime, water, sand, and oyster shells that he quarried from the ruins of Fort Frederica. For the lighting apparatus, Gould placed oil lamps suspended on chains in the lantern room.

Gould came to like the island so much that he was appointed lighthouse keeper at an annual salary of $400. He remained keeper for twenty-seven years (1810-37) and did much to make the offshore waters safe. For example, he designed an effective system of buoys offshore, a system that novelist Eugenia Price describes in her *Lighthouse* novel.

In Christ Church Cemetery near Fort Frederica, visitors can see the gravesites of some of the lighthouse keepers and their families, including keeper James Gould.

In 1857, the federal government installed a third-order, double-convex Fresnel lens in the tower to extend its range and power. During the Civil War, Confederate troops built Fort Brown nearby. When they abandoned the area in 1862, they burned down the wooden fort and dynamited the lighthouse so that federal troops could not use it.

After the war, Georgia architect Charles Cluskey designed a 104-foot-tall tower. The new lighthouse, which was finished in 1872 at a cost of $45,000, still stands. At the same time, workers built a nine-room, two-story Victorian house for the keepers and their families. The twelve-inch-thick walls of that house have successfully withstood many storms over the years.

Architect Cluskey did not live to see the completion of the tower he designed. He died in 1871 from malaria or yellow fever. Both were diseases that local residents had to contend with, since the stagnant water in ponds on the island provided a perfect breeding ground for the dreaded mosquito. Repeated requests from the lighthouse keepers finally resulted in the Lighthouse Board draining the

ponds in the winter. This greatly alleviated the problem.

Before the highway to the mainland was built in 1924, living on the island was lonely for the keepers, their families, and others who farmed and fished there. They all had to be self-sufficient, growing crops and fishing, especially since the shipment of supplies was erratic.

In 1890, workers built the fire-proof 9' by 11' brick oil-house to store a year's supply of kerosene for the tower. When the original power source, whale oil, became too expensive as whales became scarcer, the light was fueled with kerosene. In 1934, kerosene was replaced with electricity. When the last lighthouse keeper retired in the early 1950s, the tower was automated.

The original third-order Fresnel lens, which is less powerful than the first-order lens found in some towers today, projects a light that can be seen from eighteen miles out to sea on a clear night. The U.S. Coast Guard still maintains the lighthouse.

In 1972, the federal government allowed a local group to take over the unused keepers' house near the tower for a museum and visitors' center. The Coastal Georgia Historical Society, which is located on the lighthouse grounds, spent three years renovating the buildings, and opened them to the public in 1975. When officials opened the lighthouse tower to visitors in 1984, many walked up the 129 steps to see the spectacular view. Of particular interest are the ruins of the first lighthouse east of the present tower, which archaeologists excavated in 1974.

The site's Museum of Coastal History has exhibits detailing the maritime and other histories of the area, including pictures of the original lighthouse.

As with many lighthouses, St. Simon's has at least one ghost story. In March 1880, keeper Frederick Osborne was killed after a heated argument with the assistant keeper. To this day, some people claim that they can hear Osborne's footsteps in the tower, especially at night.

Nearby is Neptune Park, which honors the faithful slave, Neptune Small, who showed great

loyalty to his family during the Civil War (see Chapter 20 for details).

The downtown area is a favorite with visitors for shopping, dining, and watching the boats on St. Simons Sound.

DIRECTIONS

From Brunswick, follow signs east to St. Simons Island. Cross the causeway to the island, take the first right onto Kings Way, proceed to Mallory Street, turn right on Mallory, then left at Beach View Drive, and right onto 12th Street. The lighthouse and museum are handicap accessible. Open all year, Monday through Saturday, 10 A.M.–5 P.M.; Sunday, 1:30 P.M.–5 P.M. Closed on selected holidays. Admission fee. Phone: (912) 638-4666.

Further Reading

Betsy Fancher. *The Lost Legacy of Georgia's Golden Isles.* Garden City, NY: Doubleday, 1971, esp. pp. 143–171.

Georgia Writers' Project. "St. Simons Island." *Drums and Shadows: Survival Studies among the Georgia Coastal Negroes.* Athens, GA: University of Georgia Press, 1986, pp. 173–185.

Historic Glimpses of St. Simons Island, 1736-1924. St. Simons Island, GA: Coastal Georgia Historical Society, 1973.

Tommy E. Jenkins. *A Graphic History of St. Simons Island.* St. Simons Island, GA: Tommy E. Jenkins, 1994, esp. pp. 52–56.

Eugenia Price. *Lighthouse.* 1971; Nashville, TN: Rutledge Hill Press, 1985. [For Price's other books set on St. Simons, see bibliography in Chapter 20.]

Buddy Sullivan. "The Lighthouses of Georgia." *The Keeper's Log: The Quarterly Journal of the United States Lighthouse Society*, vol. 4, no. 3 (spring 1988), pp. 2–11.

Burnette Vanstory. "The Haunted Lighthouse." *Ghost Stories & Superstitions of Old Saint Simons.* St. Simons Island, GA: Coastal Georgia Historical Society, 1994, esp. pp. 9–10.

TWENTY-THREE

🜂 The Cloister

Sea Island

[Sea Island] delightfully combines natural and cultivated beauty, perfectly balances luxurious living and casual comfort.
— Burnette Vanstory, *Georgia's Land of the Golden Isles*

ea Island, which is about 5.1 miles long and 2.1 miles wide, was almost completely uninhabited until this century. Evidence does indicate that Native Americans lived here briefly. However, they seemed to have preferred to live on St. Simons Island, perhaps because Sea Island has more marsh than upland area, and is very susceptible to northeasters. Thus, the island remained relatively isolated until the beginning of this century when several Northerners discovered its possibilities. Today, the bridge that leads over Blackbanks River from St. Simons Island to Sea Island takes us into the entirely different world of a world-famous resort and spectacular homes.

Howard Coffin, who had made a fortune building the Hudson automobile, traveled to Savannah for an auto race in 1910. While there, he discovered the charms of Georgia. A year later, he bought Sapelo Island and began a long-term commitment that would have him shuttling back and forth between his homes in Grosse Point, Michigan, and the Georgia islands.

In 1926, Coffin bought a large plantation on the

southwestern tip of St. Simons called "Kings Retreat." He and his friend Eugene Lewis later transformed the plantation into the Sea Island Golf Club. Coffin then bought Gascoigne Bluff, which later became the Sea Island Yacht Club. His company, Sea Island Company, also paved King's Way, the first hard-surface road on St. Simons.

While exploring St. Simons, Coffin came upon another island, barely separated from the larger island by a little creek. The little island has had many names: Fifth Creek Island, Isle of Palms, Long Island, Goat Island, and Glynn Isle. Sensing the possibilities of its isolation, Coffin bought the island for $349,485.17, changed its name to Sea Island, and made plans to develop it into a hunting preserve. He later stocked it with deer, turkeys, pheasants, and other game. Hunting parties at first spent the nights in tents, a far cry from today's mansions.

At first, Coffin wanted to build a luxurious hotel on St. Simons, but an acquaintance, Carl Fisher, the developer of Miami Beach, convinced him to build it on Sea Island instead.

Coffin was undeterred by the fact that his new island, as well as nearby St. Simons, had few amenities: no electricity, no telephone service, few workers, and few supplies. Instead, as he had done in the development of the automobile, he saw an opportunity to carve out a great resort. He enlisted the help of his cousin, Alfred W. Jones, and together they made plans for the new property.

They built the mile-long causeway from St. Simons to Sea Island, installed a power plant and telephone system, and then began a golf course. For the new hotel's architect, Coffin hired the brilliant (if somewhat eccentric) Addison Mizner, who had transformed Palm Beach, Florida, into a Mediterranean-style resort for the wealthy. It was Mizner who convinced Coffin to name the new hotel "The Cloister" after Mizner's "Cloister Inn" in Boca Raton, Florida.

The landscaper was a young man in his early twenties, T. Miesse Baumgardner. Baumgardner had to adapt the hotel's grounds to its surroundings of marsh and goat pasture. The gardens that he designed blended in nicely with the Spanish architecture of the hotel.

When the luxurious hotel was completed in 1928, the developers held three openings: one for local investors, one for specially invited guests, and one for journalists and columnists. The Cloister was soon known for its upscale lifestyle and elegant surroundings, becoming a resort that some have called "the grande dame of resortdom." Even after Howard Coffin's death in 1937, Alfred W. Jones continued planning and building.

Coffin and his first wife, Matilda, are buried in the cemetery at Christ Church on St. Simons, on one of the islands he had such a role in developing. In a larger sense, The Cloister stands as his memorial.

Among The Cloister's many famous guests was playwright Eugene O'Neill, who lived on the island for five years (1931–36). He is honored with the Eugene O'Neill Oak near the hotel. O'Neill, the author of such well-known plays as *Anna Christie*, *The Emperor Jones*, *Desire Under the Elms*, and *Strange Interlude*, was the first American playwright to win the Nobel Prize for literature (1936). He also won four Pulitzer Prizes for Drama (1920, 1922, 1928, and 1957). After finishing *Mourning Becomes Electra*, he came to Sea Island with his third wife, Carlotta. They stayed at The Cloister for a month, and then decided to build their own house on the island along the ocean at Agramont (Nineteenth) Street.

They named their house Casa Genotta (**Euge**ne and Car**lotta**) and created an upstairs studio in which O'Neill could work. They soon became immersed in the island life, entertaining such guests as Sherwood Anderson, Bennett Cerf, Lillian Gish, and Somerset Maugham. While on Sea Island, O'Neill worked on three of his best-known works: *Long Day's Journey into Night*, *Days Without End*, and *Ah Wilderness*.

Other renowned hotel guests have included presidents Calvin Coolidge (who planted the Constitution Oak on the grounds of The Cloister in 1928), Dwight D. Eisenhower, Gerald Ford, Jimmy Carter, and George Bush, as well as the Netherlands' Queen Juliana (who planted the Queen's Oak in 1952).

The rest of Sea Island, which visitors can drive through on the main road, the oak-shaded Sea

Island Drive, has thirty-six blocks of spectacular homes. The street names, which commemorate Native Americans, Spaniards, pirates, and colonists, all have something to do with Georgia history.

Sea Island's beach, which is wide and beautiful, was named by readers of *Gourmet* magazine in May 1997 as one of the five best beaches in the world. However, because the island is privately owned, there is no public beach access.

Among the annual visitors to the beach are hundreds of turtles, which return during nesting season to lay their eggs.

⁂

DIRECTIONS

From St. Simons Island, continue on Frederica Road to Sea Island Drive. Follow the signs over the small bridge to Sea Island. Signs then direct visitors to The Cloister. For reservations call 1-800-732-4752 or (912) 638-3611. For information on renting homes, contact Sea Island Company, Sea Island, GA 31561; phone: (912) 638-3611.

Further Reading

Tonya D. Clayton, Lewis A. Taylor, Jr., and others. *Living with the Georgia Shore.* Durham, NC: Duke University Press, 1992, esp. pp. 90–96.

Betsy Fancher. "Sea Island: Grande Dame of Resortdom." *The Lost Legacy of Georgia's Golden Isles.* Garden City, NY: Doubleday, 1971, esp. pp. 173–181:

Don W. Farrant. *The Lure and Lore of the Golden Isles.* Nashville, TN: Rutledge Hill Press, 1993, esp. pp. 42–45 [about Eugene O'Neill].

Harold H. Martin. *This Happy Isle: The Story of Sea Island and the Cloister.* Sea Island, GA: Sea Island Company, 1978.

Buddy Sullivan. *Early Days on the Georgia Tidewater: The Story of McIntosh County and Sapelo.* 4th edition. Darien, GA: McIntosh County Commission, 1995.

Burnette Vanstory. *Georgia's Land of the Golden Isles.* Athens, GA: University of Georgia Press, 1956, esp. pp. 168–174.

*T*WENTY-FOUR

Little St. Simons Island

The trees [on Little St. Simons Island] were all strained crooked, from the constant influence of the sea blast. The coast was a fearful-looking stretch of dismal, trackless sand, and the ocean lay boundless and awful beyond the wild and desolate beach. . . .

— Fanny Kemble, *Journal of a Residence on a Georgian Plantation in 1838–1839*

*L*ittle St. Simons is a barrier island that has remained virtually unchanged for hundreds, maybe thousands, of years. Located northeast of St. Simons Island, it is accessible only by boat. The island curves like a shrimp around the northern tip of St. Simons and protects the larger island from northern storms.

Altamaha Sound separates Little St. Simons, which measures 5.2 miles long and 3.6 miles wide, from Wolf Island and Egg Island to the north, and the Hampton River separates the island from Sea Island to the south.

The island has seven miles of beautiful beaches, although relatively few people ever go there to enjoy them. Although privately owned today, the island can accommodate up to twenty-four visitors, who stay in one of the four cottages and experience one of the most pristine places on the whole Atlantic coast. A specially trained team of cooks prepares meals for the guests.

The first human residents of Little St. Simons and other Georgia barrier islands lived there at the end of the Pleistocene Epoch, ten thousand years ago. Since then, vari-

ous Native American peoples have lived, hunted, and fished on the islands. The tribes there at the time of the Spanish exploration period in the late 1500s were the Guales. Eventually, the Native Americans moved away or were killed by European diseases, weapons, or enforced slavery.

The first private owner of the island seems to have been Samuel Ougspourger (or Augspourger), a Swiss colonist who lived in South Carolina. Ougspourger bought Little St. Simons in 1760 from King George II. Eight years later, he sold it to his grandson, Gabriel Manigault of South Carolina, for the equivalent of around $17,000 in today's money.

The island's next owner was Major Pierce Butler, who bought Little St. Simons in 1784, as well as the Hampton Plantation on St. Simons. Hampton Plantation was located on Butler's Point, across the creek from Cannon's Point. It was once the site of General Oglethorpe's New Hampton outpost.

Major Butler developed the plantation into an efficient producer of cotton and rice. The flooding of the nearby Altamaha River provided the nutrients and fresh water the rice needed to thrive. (For more about Major Butler, see Chapter 17.)

Butler's wife, actress Fanny Kemble, described day-trips from Hampton to Little St. Simons, for which slaves took a horse and carriage over to the island by barge. One day-trip in particular almost did her in:

> The sun glared upon us from the cloudless sky, and the air was one cloud of sandflies and mosquitoes. I covered both my children's faces with veils and handkerchiefs, and repented not a little in my own breast of the rashness of my undertaking. The back of Israel's coat was covered so thick with mosquitoes that one could hardly see the cloth; and I felt as if we should be stifled if our way lay much longer through this terrible wood. (*Journal*, pp. 333–34)

Among Major Butler's many guests in 1804 was Aaron Burr, vice president of the United States and the man who had killed Alexander Hamilton in a duel that year. Burr had come south to escape the publicity and wait until he felt it would be safe to return north.

That same year also saw a terrible hurricane hit Little St. Simons, nearly killing more than a hundred workers in the fields. One of the overseers on the island, a man named Morris, saw the signs of the approaching storm and put all his men into a sturdy structure called a "hurricane house" just in time to save them from the fury of the storm. In gratitude for his quick thinking, the Butler family presented Morris with an engraved silver cup that has been passed down from generation to generation.

One result of the 1804 hurricane was that dikes were built on Little St. Simons to protect the rice fields from further flooding. Visitors can still see remnants of those dikes.

(An even worse hurricane, which caused much damage and killed some eighty people, was an 1898 storm that slammed into the Georgia coast and hammered it for eighteen hours. Even today, people on the island must be watchful. Since there are no roads or bridges—only boats—residents must evacuate early when a hurricane approaches.)

A few years later, during the War of 1812, the British "liberated" over a hundred of Major Butler's slaves and took them north on British ships. Many of the slaves, who eventually settled in Bermuda and Nova Scotia, kept the last name of Butler. One site that visitors can still see on Old House Road is the ruins of "Quash's House," the home of one of Major Butler's slaves who stayed on the island as a boatman and watchman.

After slavery was outlawed, the plantation owners had a difficult time tilling the soil, growing their crops, and coping with the elements. Many farms, especially the more isolated ones like those on Little St. Simons, were allowed to revert to their natural state.

The history of Little St. Simons almost took a fatal turn in the early 1900s, when O.F. Chichester of the Eagle Pencil Company visited the island and bought it. Chichester was going to harvest the trees on both Little St. Simons and Sea Island (then called Long Island) for his pencil-making business. After his workers had taken all the trees they needed, he planned to sell the islands. Without trees, the islands would probably have eroded away to nothing. Fortunately, however, the trees were too gnarled, and

Chichester realized that he could not use the wood for pencils. In 1908, he sold Little St. Simons to the Berolzheimer family.

The Berolzheimers built a bungalow on the southern end of the island and a hunting lodge in the middle, across from Cannon Point's on St. Simons. The hunting lodge became quite popular when the family stocked the island with deer, which they and their guests could hunt. The bungalow burned down in the 1930s, perhaps in a fire set by poachers or rattlesnake hunters, but the hunting lodge remained the center of the island's social life.

During World War II, soldiers and sailors patrolled the beaches, watching for submarines and landing parties, and Coast Guard vessels patrolled in the offshore waters. Later, workers deposited on the island large amounts of sediment dredged from the Intracoastal Waterway. In 1947, local African Americans tried to acquire the island as a "beach park for Negroes," but did not succeed.

Marsh makes up most of the island, only about a quarter of which is high ground. Among the additions made to the island this century have been a dock (pictured here) and bulkhead on Mosquito Creek, groves of citrus trees, and many different kinds of animals. Officials have removed some of the animals, for example the cattle, because of the damage they did to the trees and dunes.

Well-to-do guests, especially those from the political circles of New York City, have stayed on the island over the years. Former Georgia governor Jimmy Carter visited soon after his election to the presidency in 1976. This was also the year when the owners of the island opened it to the public. They could have sold Little St. Simons, the way so many owners of coastal islands have done, but instead they decided to use it for their own vacations and to make it available to a few others. Guests who make the trip to the island can enjoy horseback riding, fishing, swimming, and canoe trips. There is also excellent birdwatching: Among the many species of birds on Little St. Simons are the rare Wilson's plovers, least terns, and black-necked stilts.

Today, thanks to careful management, Fanny Kemble's description of the island in 1839 as "a small green screen of tangled wilderness" still applies.

⇗

DIRECTIONS

The ferry for Little St. Simons departs daily from the Hampton River Club Marina on the north side of St. Simons. For reservations call (912) 638-7472; FAX: (912) 634-1811. Address: Little St. Simons Island, P.O. Box 21078 NAV, St. Simons Island, GA 31522.

Further Reading

Margaret Armstrong. *Fanny Kemble: A Passionate Victorian.* New York: Macmillan Co., 1938.

Malcolm Bell, Jr. *Major Butler's Legacy: Five Generations of a Slaveholding Family.* Athens, GA: University of Georgia Press, 1987.

Tonya D. Clayton, Lewis A. Taylor, Jr., and others. *Living with the Georgia Shore.* Durham, NC: Duke University Press, 1992, esp. pp. 88–90.

Fanny Kemble. *Journal of a Residence on a Georgian Plantation in 1838–1839.* New York: Knopf, 1961.

Junius Rochester. *Little St. Simons Island on the Coast of Georgia.* Place?: Little St. Simons Press, 1994.

Buddy Sullivan. *Early Days on the Georgia Tidewater: The Story of McIntosh County and Sapelo.* 4th edition. Darien, GA: McIntosh County Commission, 1995.

$\mathcal{T}$WENTY-FIVE

❧ The Jekyll Island Club

Jekyll Island

[Jekyll Island Club is the] richest, the most exclusive, the most inaccessible club in the world.
— Munsey Magazine, 1904

$\mathcal{T}$he coastal lands were too rich in wildlife and beaches, and had too good a climate to remain isolated for long. In time, wealthy European and northern industrialists discovered what the Native Americans had known 4,500 years ago: Coastal Georgia has great natural beauty.

Georgia was far enough away from the industrialized Northeast to retain much of its frontier status well into the nineteenth century. But once the steamer and train made it accessible, the floodgates were opened by tourists and settlers alike. When the airplane and automobile came along, they made even more people aware of the Peach State. To make sure that some of the Georgia islands would remain open only to the wealthy and their friends, a number of northern industrialists bought several of them and made them their exclusive domain.

One of these, Jekyll Island, has had a checkered history: Native Americans used it as a hunting grounds, the English settled it, the Spanish laid claim to it, and a French family owned it at one time. The island was named by General

Oglethorpe, founder of Georgia, for Sir Joseph Jekyll, an early English financier of the colony. Some claim the name goes back to a Frenchman named Jacque (thus "Jacque's Island" or "Jake's Isle" or "Jakyll"), who operated a supply station for local pirates in the 1600s.

The island had a plantation run by Captain (later Major) William Horton, one of Oglethorpe's aides, who brewed beer on Jekyll for the English troops at Fort Frederica. Horton eventually took command of the English forces when Oglethorpe returned to England.

The Spanish destroyed much of Horton's plantation when they invaded the island after the English had beaten them in the Battle of Bloody Marsh on St. Simons Island in 1742, but Horton later rebuilt his house and by 1746, he had restored his plantation.

After the Revolutionary War, a French family, the du Bignons, took over the island and controlled it for a century. They grew cotton on its 11,000 acres and thus prospered until well into the 1800s. Members of the family, who came to America in the early 1790s after fleeing the French Revolution, are buried across the road from William Horton's house on North Riverview Drive.

Visitors can see on the northern part of the island the two-story ruins of the du Bignon House, which was built on the foundation of Horton's tabby house. The ruin, dating from 1742, is one of the state's oldest tabby structures still standing. Across the road is a wall, all that remains today of Georgia's first brewery.

Descendants of the du Bignon family eventually sold the island in 1886 for $125,000 to a group of wealthy capitalists who wanted to escape the cold northern winters and head south for hunting on a private island. The Jekyll Island Club, which they established in 1886, had as members some of the wealthiest businessmen in America, for example the Astors, Goulds, Morgans, Rockefellers, and Vanderbilts. Some writers estimate that the exclusive group controlled one-sixth of the world's wealth at that time.

What the industrialists found on this island was a refuge from their problems, pristine surroundings, and a chance to hunt and fish with like-minded elite. The members, who often bequeathed their cottages to their descendants rather than sell them to the highest bidder, were not allowed to publicize club activities. This gave the club even more exclusivity.

The size of the island (7.4 miles long and 2.3 miles wide) and its inaccessibility from the mainland (one river and four miles of marsh away) made it ideal, even though only about two-thirds of the island was usable (the rest was marsh).

For those who did not have their own cottages (see the next chapter), the turreted, four-story clubhouse had sixty rooms to accommodate visitors. The elaborate dining room served elegant meals, which were prepared by a chef and full staff from Delmonico's of New York.

The clubhouse served more than food one day in 1899, when a political scandal nearly erupted between President William McKinley, who was about to seek a second term in the White House, and Speaker of the House Thomas Reed, who opposed McKinley. Senator Mark Hanna, a very powerful political leader at that time, was supposed to help the two men settle their differences and decide who should become the next president.

When the president's party, including McKinley, his vice president, and members of his cabinet, arrived in Brunswick in five very luxurious railroad cars, the people on the mainland knew something was up. But, like the rest of the country, the outsiders could find out nothing about what was going on, despite the fact that one of the most important newspapermen of the time, Joseph Pulitzer of the *New York World*, was also staying on the island.

L.J. Leavy, a young reporter for the Brunswick newspaper, somehow learned details from a secret source, which later turned out to be one of the women who knew what was going on at the meeting. He wired the story around the country, scooping all the major newspapers. The unwanted publicity forced the politicians on the island to call off the deal and return to Washington. Reed was ousted as

Speaker of the House, and McKinley won a second term as president.

A more praiseworthy meeting took place at the club in 1910, when a banking committee, composed of many of the most important financiers of the day, met there to discuss the country's financial situation. Their conclusions, after ten days of deliberation, resulted in what was called the "Aldrich Plan." That plan evolved into the Federal Reserve System, which revamped the banking system and led to better financial conditions for everyone.

The club died out in the 1930s when the heirs of the founders discovered south Florida as a winter retreat. Later, World War II greatly reduced the supply of available local labor that was needed to maintain the facilities on Jekyll Island. As a result, the club disbanded in 1942. Five years later, the State of Georgia bought the island for a state park for only $675,000.

At that time, visitors had to make the trip by boat either from the mainland or from St. Simons Island. By 1954, when a causeway and bridge connected Jekyll Island to the mainland, the not-so-rich-and-famous could visit one of the best-managed islands on the Atlantic coast. For a while, the clubhouse operated as a hotel, but it soon deteriorated. It seemed destined for the wrecker's ball, but a group of investors leased and renovated it. Later, the hotel became part of the Radisson franchise.

Today, the renamed "Jekyll Island Club Hotel" retains much of its former elegance. Guests play croquet on the lawn and dine formally in the Grand Dining Room, where the millionaires once had their meals, since many of their cottages did not have proper kitchens. And if the hotel no longer has living Vanderbilts there, it does serve a "Vanderbilt" for breakfast, a croissant stuffed with scrambled eggs.

The one-time stable for the Jekyll Island Club is today a Museum Visitor Center with exhibits, maps, and information on the tours of the island, especially its National Historic Landmark District. The island has the state's largest public golf facility, with three eighteen-hole courses and one nine-hole course. Other amenities include the Tennis Center with seven lighted courts, several campgrounds, a water park, and a convention center. The island also has twenty miles of level, paved bicycle/jogging paths.

DIRECTIONS

From I-95 take U.S. 31 or 84 to State Road 50 and follow signs for the causeway to Jekyll Island. For information about the island tours call 1-800-982-9332. For information about the golf courses call (912) 635-2368 or 635-3464 or 635-2170. For reservations at the Jekyll Island Club Hotel call 1-800-535-9547 or (912) 635-2600. The Jekyll Island Welcome Center (1-800-841-6586) also has good information.

Further Reading

Betsy Fancher. *The Lost Legacy of Georgia's Golden Isles.* Garden City, NY: Doubleday, 1971, esp. pp. 183–193.

Don W. Farrant. *The Lure and Lore of the Golden Isles.* Nashville, TN: Rutledge Hill Press, 1993.

Burnette Vanstory. *Georgia's Land of the Golden Isles.* Athens, GA: University of Georgia Press, 1956, esp. pp. 175–181.

William Barton McCash and June Hall McCash. *The Jekyll Island Club: Southern Haven for America's Millionaires.* Athens, GA: University of Georgia Press, 1989.

n 1798, Georgia outlawed the importation of slaves

TWENTY-SIX

↬ Millionaires' Village

Jekyll Island

> *Millionaires' Village on Jekyll Island is a monument to the greatest single conservation tool to benefit the Georgia coast, the acquisitive powers of northern industrial wealth.*
> — *Coastal Georgia*

*T*from Africa. By 1808, importing slaves into the United States was a federal offense. But because the maze of small islands and creeks along the Georgia coast made slave smuggling easy for skilled mariners, Jekyll and other islands became landing sites for slavers.

In trying to escape bondage, slaves sometimes resorted to drastic measures, including mass suicide. One legend of nearby St. Simons Island says that a group of slaves who arrived at Ebo Landing shackled together chose to die by drowning rather than remain in slavery.

Just before dawn broke on November 29, 1858, the slave ship *Wanderer* landed on the shore of Jekyll Island with what turned out to be the last major illegal importation of slaves into this country. The 409 slaves had survived a horrendous forty-day trip across the Atlantic. The storm that drove the ship ashore allowed some of the slaves to escape, and for years afterward, African Americans on Jekyll Island claimed to be descendants of those escaped slaves. The owners of the ship were caught and prosecuted, but the landing on Jekyll pointed out how remote such sites were.

Later, near where those slaves landed, some of the richest businessmen in our country built vacation homes. These were the men who made Jekyll into one of the most exclusive private hunting refuges on the Georgia coast.

When they bought Jekyll Island in 1886, these industrialists built an exquisite clubhouse for themselves and invited guests. Some also built their own seasonal houses, even though they would stay on the island with their families for only three months, usually from mid-January to Easter.

The small mansions, which they modestly called "cottages," that the families built on the western shore of the island near the Inland Waterway were very elegant, and in some cases very extravagant. Today, those who visit the Jekyll Island Club Historic District, formerly called "Millionaires' Village," can tour those cottages that have survived storms and deterioration. Some have been restored to their former splendor.

What follows is a representative sample and brief description of some of the cottages: (Refer to the numbered map.) Located just to the south of (1) the Jekyll Island Club Hotel is (2) **Indian Mound/Rockefeller Cottage**. The first part of the cottage's name refers to the mound of shells on the front lawn. The twenty-five-room house was built in

1892 by inventor/industrialist Gordon McKay of Pittsfield, Massachusetts. McKay, who had made his fortune during the Civil War by mass-producing well-made boots for soldiers, had divorced his first wife in the 1840s, married his housekeeper's daughter in 1878, and divorced her in 1890. However, he was so fond of his second wife that he gave her and her German husband $100,000 as a wedding gift.

William Rockefeller, younger brother of oilman John D. Rockefeller and president of the Standard Oil Company of New York, bought Indian Mound Cottage in 1904. Rockefeller was particularly happy on Jekyll and spent much time there, even after his wife died at Indian Mound in 1920, two years before he died in New York. Among the objects that visitors can see on display at Indian Mound Cottage are several from playwright Eugene O'Neill's home on Sea Island to the north.

Near Indian Mound/Rockefeller Cottage is a replica of a telephone through which Theodore Vail, first president of AT&T, took part in 1915 in what was supposedly the first transcontinental phone conversation. The call included President Woodrow Wilson in Washington, Alexander Graham Bell in New York, Thomas Watson in San Francisco (Bell's assistant who answered Bell's first telephone transmittal: "Mr. Watson, come here. I want you."), and

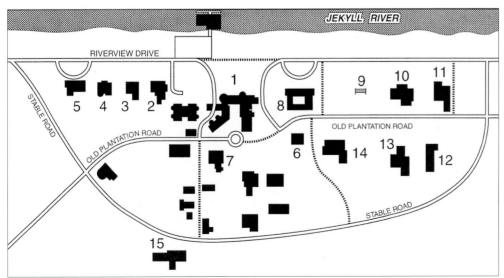

(1) Jekyll Island Club
(2) Indian Mound/
    Rockefeller Cottage
(3) Mistletoe Cottage
(4) Goodyear Cottage
(5) Moss/Macy Cottage
(6) Faith Chapel
(7) duBignon Cottage
(8) Crane Cottage
(9) Chicota Cottage
(10) Hollybourne
(11) Villa Ospo
(12) Gould Casino
(13) Villa Marianna
(14) Cherokee Cottage
(15) Visitor Center

Mr. Vail on Jekyll Island. To allow Vail, who was recuperating at Jekyll from an ankle injury, to be part of the call, workers had laid a thousand miles of cable between New York and the island.

(3) **Mistletoe Cottage**, just to the south of Indian Mound Cottage, was built in 1900 in the Dutch Colonial Revival style for Henry Porter of Pittsburgh, the manufacturer of light locomotives.

(4) **Goodyear Cottage**, further south, was built in 1906 for lumber and railroad man Frank Goodyear of Buffalo, New York. The house was restored in 1974 and is now used for the Center for the Creative Arts with exhibits of regional artists.

(5) **Moss/Macy Cottage**, next door to Goodyear Cottage, was built in 1896 for William Struthers, owner of a Philadelphia marble works. It was later owned by George Macy, who was president of what became the Atlantic & Pacific Tea Company, known familiarly as the A&P.

(6) **Faith Chapel** stands northeast of the Jekyll Island Club Hotel. The chapel was built in 1904 and is best-known for its Tiffany stained-glass window. Ministers used the chapel to give sermons on such subjects as "It is only to the man of morality that wealth comes," which the millionaires liked to hear.

(7) The **du Bignon Cottage**, south of Faith Chapel, was not one of the original cottages; it was already on the site when Eugene du Bignon and Newton Finney sold Jekyll Island to the Club.

(8) **Crane Cottage**, to the north of the hotel, is a large, 1917 Italian Renaissance-style residence with a large kitchen and seventeen bathrooms. The owner of the house, the most expensive ever built on the island, was Richard Teller Crane of Chicago, the manufacturer of bathroom fixtures.

(9) **Chichota Cottage**, which once stood to the north, is marked by two stone lions. Chichota fell into disrepair after the owners had lost their son in a tragic hunting accident on the island, and was torn down.

(10) **Hollybourne** or **Charles Maurice Cottage**, next to Chichota, was built in 1890 for Charles Maurice, a well-known bridge engineer. It was the only cottage made of tabby.

(11) **Villa Ospo**, also known as the **Jennings Cottage**, is to the north along Riverview Drive. The cottage was built in 1928 for Walter Jennings, one of the first directors of the Standard Oil Company of New Jersey.

(12) **Gould Casino** (with an indoor tennis court), (13) **Villa Marianna** (now a private residence with an outdoor fountain of beautiful Spanish tiles), and (14) **Shrady-James/Cherokee Cottage** (named in honor of the Cherokee Rose, Georgia's state flower) are located on Old Plantation Road.

The families who built these beautiful houses also built such amenities as a golf course near the beach across the island. The families continued to come to the island until the end of 1941. But the demands of World War II (gas rationing, curtailed travel for most Americans, labor scarcity, and the potential threat of German submarines off the coast) effectively ended what had been over five decades of vacationing at an exclusive resort.

Today, some eight hundred permanent residents live on the island. The homes outside of the Historic District are privately owned; owners pay a land-lease fee to the Jekyll Island Authority under a ninety-nine-year lease, which is transferable when the ownership of the house changes. No more lots are available for building.

Visitors can learn more about the cottages, including how to rent some of them for weddings and receptions, at (15) the Museum Visitor Center, which is open daily from 9:30 A.M. to 4 P.M. Call (912) 635-4036 for information.

DIRECTIONS

Begin by following Riverview Drive south of the Jekyll Island Club Hotel, which is in the Historic District and facing the Marina on Jekyll Creek.

Further Reading

Betsy Fancher. *The Lost Legacy of Georgia's Golden Isles*. Garden City, NY: Doubleday, 1971, esp. pp. 183–193.

Don W. Farrant. *The Lure and Lore of the Golden Isles*. Nashville, TN: Rutledge Hill Press, 1993.

Burnette Vanstory. *Georgia's Land of the Golden Isles*. Athens, GA: University of Georgia Press, 1956, esp. pp. 175–181.

William Barton McCash and June Hall McCash. *The Jekyll Island Club: Southern Haven for America's Millionaires*. Athens, GA: University of Georgia Press, 1989.

$\mathcal{T}$WENTY-SEVEN

∾ Lighthouse

Little Cumberland Island

At the start of World War II all but two [Tybee and St. Simons] of Georgia's light stations had been deactivated by the Lighthouse Service due to a severe decline in trade and the resultant decrease in shipping traffic at the smaller ports.

— Buddy Sullivan, *Lighthouses of Georgia*

$\mathcal{L}$ittle Cumberland Island is located on St. Andrew Sound, north of Cumberland Island. Unlike the more developed barrier islands (Jekyll, Sea, St. Simons, and Tybee), this island has seen few settlers. Nevertheless, it too shows some of the effects of human habitation.

Because the island is part of the Coastal Barrier Resources System and three-quarters of it is designated as wilderness, its development is limited. The island does, however, have one hundred privately owned lots, each about two acres in size. Development of these lots is governed by strict rules, and owners can only build single-unit dwellings.

The 2.4-mile-long island lies south of St. Andrew Sound and north of Cumberland Island. The Cumberland River is to the west and the Atlantic to the east. Two creeks, Christmas and Brockington, intersect the island, making much of it marshy, a condition that further limits its development. Different sections of Little Cumberland are subject to erosion or build-up, depending on where they are in relation to the wind and tides.

In 1802, the state government gave jurisdiction over six acres on the southern end of the main (Great) Cumberland Island to the U.S. government so the federal government could build a lighthouse there. Eighteen years later, officials authorized Winslow Lewis to build a seventy-four-foot tower on this, the southernmost point of the Georgia coast. That lighthouse functioned well until 1838.

But in the mid-1830s, officials decided to build a lighthouse on the northern end of Little Cumberland Island. Joseph Hastings of Boston built the sixty-foot-tall brick structure, along with a keeper's house. The tower's diameter tapered upward from twenty-two feet at the base to eleven feet at the top. It had a stationary light, as distinguished from the revolving light in use on the tower on Great Cumberland Island.

In June 1838, the new tower, sometimes called the St. Andrews Lighthouse, began operating. That same year, workers dismantled the lighthouse on Cumberland Island and transported it down the coast to Fernandina, Florida, where it still operates on Amelia Island.

The first lighthouse keeper on Little Cumberland was David Thompson, who earned $400 annually and kept the position for eleven years.

Because the island was so small, some of the early lighthouse keepers lived on Great Cumberland Island and farmed the land there in addition to maintaining the new lighthouse.

The tower on Little Cumberland was not damaged during the Civil War, possibly because it wasn't functioning at the time. In 1867, workers installed a third-order Fresnel lens and relit the lighthouse. Although most of the post-Civil War keepers lasted for only a short time each (some of them just a few months), one of them, Henry Swan, maintained the lighthouse for ten years (1874-84).

Several large rice plantations developed along the Satilla River on the mainland to the west of Little Cumberland, doing much to help the economy of surrounding Camden County. The plantations greatly increased the water traffic in the vicinity. The lighthouse was probably used as a reckoning point for slave smugglers. West of the lighthouse, for

example, and near Woodbine, was a prison in which slave owners chained those slaves newly arrived from Africa. The purpose was to confine the slaves with iron rings that were fastened in the floor until the owners could make them more manageable. Later, the owners would put the new slaves in the field where more experienced slaves could teach them how to work in the rice fields.

That particular lighthouse must have seen much smuggling of slaves and contraband into southern Georgia. From the testimony from former slaves recorded in *Drums and Shadows: Survival Studies among the Georgia Coastal Negroes*, we can see how the waters off Little Cumberland Island must have been very busy. In fact, in Camden County, the slave population represented 76% of the county's total population in 1860.

Not all the slaves made it to shore, however. As reported by Julia Floyd Smith in her book *Slavery and Rice Culture in Low Country Georgia*, sometimes a slave ship's crew would throw their human cargo overboard to get rid of the evidence of their illicit trade, especially if they were being pursued by a naval patrol off the Georgia coast.

One of the plantations on the mainland, Refuge Plantation, was one of the largest in the South. The McIntosh family owned the plantation, first George in 1765 and then his son, John Houston McIntosh. John's daughter, Eliza Bayard McIntosh, married the Seminole War hero, General Duncan Lamont Clinch, and they settled there in 1836. Their family kept the plantation until 1905.

However, as plantations like Refuge began to rely less on water and more on other means for transporting their produce, and as the abolition of slavery stopped a source of cheap labor necessary for the rice cultivation, fewer ships used the Satilla. Perhaps if Woodbine Plantation farther up the Satilla had become larger, more ships might have used St. Andrew Sound, but that did not happen.

The Lighthouse Service finally decided that the decreased use of the Satilla made the lighthouse unnecessary, and deactivated it in 1915.

For a while, it seemed as if the encroaching ocean might topple the unused tower, but workers shored up its base with a brick wall and stabilized it. Today, the Little Cumberland Island Association owns the tower and the island.

Since 1736, the state has had fifteen lighthouses along its one-hundred-mile-long coast, but time, war, erosion, and changing economic fortunes of the different counties have taken their toll. Little Cumberland Island Lighthouse is one of five still standing along the Georgia coast, although only two (Tybee and St. Simons) remain functional. The Little Cumberland tower is probably the least visible, both because its island is privately owned and because foliage and trees have grown up around it.

DIRECTIONS

Because the island is privately owned, visitors must obtain special permission from the Little Cumberland Island Association. Those on the island must pay special attention to weather forecasts, since they must evacuate by boat. No bridge or causeway joins the island to any other land mass.

Further Reading

David L. Cipra. "The Confederate States Light House Bureau." *The Keeper's Log* [United States Lighthouse Society]. vol. 8, no. 2 (Winter 1992), pp. 6–13.

Georgia Writers' Project. *Drums and Shadows: Survival Studies among the Georgia Coastal Negroes.* Athens, GA: University of Georgia Press, 1986.

Tonya D. Clayton, Lewis A. Taylor, Jr., and others. *Living with the Georgia Shore.* Durham, NC: Duke University Press, 1992.

Julia Floyd Smith. *Slavery and Rice Culture in Low Country Georgia, 1750–1860.* Knoxville: University of Tennessee Press, 1985, esp. p. 102.

Buddy Sullivan, "The Lighthouses of Georgia," *The Keeper's Log: The Quarterly Journal of the United States Lighthouse Society,* vol. 4, no. 3 (Spring 1988), pp. 2–11.

$\mathcal{T}$WENTY-EIGHT

➷ Dungeness

Cumberland Island

Cumberland is the most brooding and mysterious of Georgia's barrier islands.
— Robert Coram, "Our National Seashore"

$\mathcal{C}$umberland is Georgia's southernmost, largest, longest island (sixteen miles long and three miles at its widest point). Its earliest inhabitants were probably the Timucuan tribe (four thousand years ago), but the island today has very few traces of the Native Americans. More recent residents were the Spanish in the 1500s, the English in the 1700s, and Americans from the 1800s on. American plantation owners used some five hundred slaves to grow sugar cane, cotton, and timber on Cumberland, but the plantations couldn't continue to run after the Civil War freed the slaves.

The island has been called by several names: "Missoe" (sassafras) by the Timucuans, "San Pedro" by Spanish missionaries, and finally "Cumberland" by the English. The English named the island for William Augustus, the young Duke of Cumberland who befriended the nephew of Chief Tomochichi when the Native Americans visited England in 1734. The young nephew asked that the island's name honor his new friend from England. Fort William, also called "Prince William's Fort," at the southern end of the island also commemorates the young duke.

The English built Fort St. Andrews at the northern edge. This fort became the center of Barrimacke, a small settlement of Scots. In 1736, General Oglethorpe built a hunting lodge at the southern end and called it "Dungeness" after the county seat of the County of Kent in England.

In the 1760s land grants on the island were made to Jonathan and Josiah Bryan (who soon owned most of the island), James Cuthbert, James Habersham, and John Smith. When naturalist William Bartram visited Cumberland in 1774, very few people lived there, although smugglers liked to use it to bring in contraband.

Dungeness became the home of the family of General Nathanael Greene, one of the heroes of the American Revolutionary War. Unfortunately, Greene died before he could finish building his home there. Ten years later, his widow married Phineas Miller, and they built a four-story house at the site that they also called "Dungeness." The mansion had four huge chimneys that served sixteen fireplaces, and its tabby walls were six feet thick. Around it were twelve acres of gardens. For the next fifty years, the house saw many splendid parties and galas.

During the War of 1812, English troops took possession of Cumberland Island and used Dungeness for their headquarters. One of the English officers, Captain Fraser, eventually married a young American belle he met on the island.

Among the many famous guests at Dungeness was General "Lighthorse" Harry Lee, the officer who wrote the definitive line of praise for George Washington: "First in war, first in peace, and first in the hearts of his countrymen."

When Lee died at Dungeness in 1818, he was buried in the little cemetery nearby. His son, General Robert E. Lee, had a tombstone placed over the grave and visited the place several times. Officials eventually had the father's body taken in 1913 to Lexington, Virginia, to lie beside the body of his son, Robert E. Lee, but visitors can still see the tombstone, which was left behind at Dungeness to commemorate the great friend of General Washington.

During the Civil War, the Dungeness mansion deteriorated, and the family moved away. The building eventually burned in 1866.

In 1881, Thomas Carnegie, steelmaker Andrew Carnegie's younger brother, bought four thousand acres of Cumberland and by 1900 owned ninety percent of it. Among the mansions built by the Carnegies were Greyfield (now an inn), Plum Orchard (administered by the National Park Service), and Dungeness (a forty-four-room, turreted Scottish castle with a pool house, squash court, and forty other buildings that accommodated the staff of three hundred). Carnegie built his Dungeness (pictured here) on the same site as the others of the same name.

The Carnegies' yacht was also called *Dungeness*, and a musician composed "Waltz Dungeness" in honor of the great house.

The wedding of Carnegie's granddaughter, Nancy, in the late 1920s may have been the last big celebration there. Much of the house was destroyed by fire in 1959, but the ruins can still convey some idea of the lavish lifestyle lived by the Carnegies and their friends.

When a developer tried to buy the island in the 1960s and turn it into another Hilton Head, landowners banded together and proposed that the U.S. Park Service buy much of the island to preserve it for future generations. In 1971, descendants of the Carnegies donated Plum Orchard and twelve surrounding acres to the National Park Foundation. Eleven years later, Congress set aside as official wilderness nearly half of the island, including Plum Orchard, which has been allowed to deteriorate, despite the efforts of at least one Carnegie descendant to make it into an artists' colony.

In 1981, the National Park Service proposed to expand the island's facilities and increase the number of visitors, but so many environmentalists opposed this plan that the Park Service backed down and agreed to preserve the natural habitat as a National Seashore. The Park Service does, however, intend to lease the Plum Orchard house to anyone who will pay for the cost of renovation.

Visitors can see abundant wildlife on the

island, ranging from loggerhead turtles on the north-end beaches to wild turkeys, wild horses, and burros. There are also, lined up in a row, some of the rusted 1920s automobiles that residents used in earlier times.

According to island legend, visitors can sometimes hear the sound of carriage wheels approaching Dungeness. The guests riding in it were supposedly killed when the carriage was wrecked long ago en route to a party.

Today, the island still has small areas that are in private hands, for example, the Greyfield Inn. The National Park Service administers the rest of the island and operates a ferry service for the three hundred visitors it allows on the island each day. No private vehicles or pets are allowed. Visitors must make reservations well in advance. They can camp in one of the restricted campsites or stay in the Greyfield Inn. The island has no stores, so visitors should bring their own food, drinks, insect repellent, suntan lotion, rain gear, film, and sunglasses.

Finally, a note about a nearby island with an unusual name: Legend has it that when nosy people asked what the moonshiners were doing on the island near the main part of Cumberland, they would be told, "Hush Your Mouth!" This was a perfectly good reason for calling the place "Hush Your Mouth Island."

DIRECTIONS

For more information about the ferry schedule and fees for Cumberland, which can be reached only by boat or plane, contact Cumberland Island National Seashore, P.O. Box 806, St. Marys, GA 31558; (912) 882-4336. For details on staying at the Greyfield Inn and its ferry service for guests, write P.O. Box 900, Fernandina Beach, FL 32035; (912) 267-0180. Website for Cumberland Island with information on lodging and ferries: http://www.gacoast.com/navigator/cumberland.html

Further Reading

Larry F. Andrews, H. Grant Rice, and Joanne C. Werwie. *Cumberland Island: A Treasure of Memories.* Tampa, FL: World-Wide Publications, 1986.

Jonathan Bryan. *Journal of a Visit to the Georgia Islands of St. Catharines, Green, Ossabaw, Sapelo, St. Simons, Jekyll, and Cumberland.* Macon, GA: Mercer University Press, 1996.

James Conaway. "Nurture vs. Nature" [about Cumberland Island]. *Preservation,* vol. 49, no. 2 (March/April 1997), pp. 40–51.

Robert Coram. "Our National Seashore." *Audubon,* vol. 96, no. 3 (May-June 1944), pp. 38–47.

Betsy Fancher. *The Lost Legacy of Georgia's Golden Isles.* Garden City, NY: Doubleday, 1971, esp. pp. 195–208.

Don W. Farrant. *The Lure and Lore of the Golden Isles.* Nashville, TN: Rutledge Hill Press, 1993.

Burnette Vanstory. *Georgia's Land of the Golden Isles.* Athens, GA: University of Georgia Press, 1956, esp. pp. 182–191.

First African Baptist Church

Cumberland Island

> *Life on the island presented an endless series of potential crises: gross tyranny, petty deceits and thievery, lying and cheating, fighting, too much rain, too little rain, the cotton worm, tornadoes, malaria, dysentery, the "black vomit" (yellow fever), dangers of snake bite, the punishing summer heat, overexhaustion, old age, imbecilism, and death.*
> — Mary Bullard, *Robert Stafford of Cumberland Island*

hen John F. Kennedy, Jr., the son of President John F. Kennedy and Jacqueline Kennedy Onassis, wed Carolyn Bessette on Cumberland Island in the fall of 1996, reporters and most others were taken by surprise. Why did Kennedy choose that windswept barrier island when he could have chosen any city in the world for his wedding? And why the small, African-American church on the island's north end? Some of Cumberland's forty thousand annual visitors must have noticed the small, isolated church built more than a century ago by freed slaves, but they probably would never have guessed the importance of its history, nor how famous it would become.

In the early 1800s, Cumberland Island planters grew excellent sea-island cotton, so called because its primary area of cultivation was on the sea islands of South Carolina and Georgia. The crop could earn up to five times the price of ordinary, short-staple cotton, but it took just the right circumstances for its cultivation. Overplanting and careful fertilizing were just two of the problems it presented.

Cotton planters on Cumberland, such as Robert Stafford, solved those problems by rotating their crops and using the rich marsh mud found on the island. Something else the farmers needed, the cyclical flooding over the fields, was more easily accomplished on the mainland plantations west of Cumberland, which were situated near fresh-water rivers. Farmers on Cumberland, which had very little fresh water, had a more difficult task flooding their fields.

The back-breaking task of carting marsh mud by buckets and oxen, as well as the planting, weeding, and cultivating, was done by slaves, of course. To keep those slaves healthy, and therefore more productive, was a responsibility the overseers on Cumberland took very seriously, not so much for humanitarian reasons as for practical reasons: Sick or dying slaves could not help grow the cotton.

One example of the overseers' "solicitude" for their slaves concerned the weekly inspection that many of the masters conducted to check on the health of the workers. On a regular basis, often on Sunday morning, the overseer would visit the slaves' houses and make sure that all the slaves were clean, that their houses were scrubbed, including the tables, dressers, and even the pails, and that the chimneys were swept. He would have the slaves gather up the fireplace ashes, which he would then use for fertilizer on the fields.

The overseer had the slaves save their oyster shells until he could burn them to make whitewash for the slaves' houses, inside and out. That practice gave a uniform color to the houses and preserved the wooden structures from insects. He also made sure the well water was clean and healthful.

Some owners gave their slaves a weekly allowance of corn or potatoes, allowing them to cook the food the way they wanted. Others, fearful that the slaves would trade away their allotment of corn or potatoes for liquor or tobacco, had their supervisors appoint one person to cook the food and distribute it to the slaves.

Some of the more enlightened owners would actually provide a nursery (and nurse) for the infant slave children, thus caring for their health needs and ensuring that they got proper amounts of food. This was safer than relying on parents who might steal the food from their infants in order to satisfy their own wants. Such "solicitude" of course resulted in more slaves and healthier workers for the fields.

With the outbreak of the Civil War in the early 1860s, slave owners fled with their families and slaves to the mainland to escape the approaching Union forces and to avoid deprivation brought on by the Union blockade that was effectively closing down the Georgia coast.

The Civil War affected plantation owners in Georgia differently. Some slave owners freed their slaves even before Lincoln's Emancipation Proclamation and helped them establish their own farms. Other owners hired their former slaves, allowing the slave families to live together and have their own plots of land. Others, angered by the war, mistreated their slaves. For example, the previously mentioned Robert Stafford burned his slave cabins and forced his workers to the northern part of the island, where they lived in primitive palmetto huts.

General Sherman of the Union army issued an order that promised the freed slaves forty-acre plots of land on the abandoned coastal islands, but that order was never effectively enforced. In any case, many former slaves eventually made their way back to Cumberland after the war and established their own settlements.

One particular place on the island where the freed slaves settled was at Brick Hill Plantation, in the middle of the island. There the African Americans could be by themselves, practice their own customs, even speak their own language, Gullah, a mixture of African languages and English. In 1893, these men and women established the First African Baptist Church, building a one-room log cabin that they used for church services and as a school. The First African Baptist Church thus represents a close link to the days of slavery. The original cabin lasted until 1937, when the parishioners built the present wood-frame church pictured here.

The new church, which the National Park Service maintains in a section of the island's north end called "Halfmoon Bluff," was carefully built. It

has eleven handmade pews which can seat a total of thirty or forty people. It has three windows on each side and at the rear.

The makeshift pulpit has an American Standard Bible that was donated in 1978 by the family of Sam Candler. The Candler family, which comes from Atlanta, became wealthy from its investment in Coca-Cola. The family owns High Point Plantation on the northern end of the island and uses the church occasionally for family services.

Most of the African Americans who used to attend the First African Baptist Church on a regular basis have moved to the mainland looking for jobs or have died.

One of the very few persons who still lives in that part of the island, in a place that is also called the "Settlement" and which used to have many descendants of the slaves living there, is researcher Carol Ruckdeschel. Her job is to collect the animals that wash up on the island and report to the Smithsonian's Museum of Natural History. She also founded Defenders of Wild Cumberland to prohibit or control development.

How, or even if, the island was to be developed became a vital issue in this century, especially when developers began making offers to the owners of Cumberland Island. What finally convinced the different owners to act together was when one-fifth of Cumberland was bought by Charles Fraser, the developer of Hilton Head, South Carolina. In a remarkable act of thoughtfulness towards future generations, the owners proposed that the island become a national seashore and remain a wilderness area. No causeway and bridge would join it to the mainland.

The federal government agreed with the owners, bought the island, including Fraser's holdings, and established Cumberland Island National Seashore in 1972. One direct result of that action is that nature is reclaiming much of the island, even the formerly inhabited part, and structures like Duck House, an abandoned hunting lodge. Large sand dunes are forming. Wildlife roams throughout the island.

Grand Avenue, the island's main connector and still, despite its name, basically a dirt road, runs almost the entire sixteen-mile length of Cumberland. Its canopy of live-oak branches, complete with Spanish moss and resurrection fern, is spectacular.

The scene on September 21, 1996 must have seemed quite out of character with the simplicity of the surroundings. Carolyn Bessette with her $40,000 gown and John F. Kennedy, Jr. in his well-tailored suit stepped out of the church onto a piece of tin that someone had placed there to ensure dry shoes in the rainy weather.

The wedding party stayed in the Greyfield Inn at the southern end of the island. (Greyfield is a raised plantation house originally built for one of the Carnegies around 1900. See Chapter 28.) It has seen many wedding parties, though probably none as elegant as the Kennedys'. Most island weddings take place at the ruins of the Dungeness mansion, the porches of Plum Orchard mansion, or the beach, usually not at the First African Baptist Church.

So why did Kennedy choose that small church? Perhaps for its isolation from curious onlookers, its link to the past, its uniqueness.

DIRECTIONS

The First African Baptist Church is at the northern part of the island. For more information about the ferry schedule and fees for Cumberland, see Chapter 28.

Further Reading

Mary R. Bullard, *An Abandoned Black Settlement on Cumberland Island, Georgia.* South Dartmouth, MA: M.R. Bullard, 1982.

Mary R. Bullard. *Black Liberation on Cumberland Island in 1815.* DeLeon Springs, FL: M.R. Bullard, 1983.

Mary R. Bullard. *Robert Stafford of Cumberland Island: Growth of a Planter.* South Dartmouth, MA: M. R. Bullard, 1986.

John E. Ehrenhard and Mary R. Bullard. *Stafford Plantation, Cumberland Island National Seashore, Georgia: Archeological Investigations of a Slave Cabin.* Tallahassee, FL: Southeast Archeological Center, National Park Service, U.S. Dept. of the Interior, 1981.

Susan P. Respess, "Cumberland Camelot" [about the Kennedy wedding], *Georgia Journal*, (November/ December 1996), pp. 28–29. [Article also has details about how to get married on Cumberland.]

THIRTY

❧ First Presbyterian Church

St. Marys

"I see you have the British crown," said a British soldier to a local
resident in St. Marys about her carpet.
"Yes, but you see it is under our feet."
— Story about St. Marys under British rule in the War of 1812

W hy would the smugglers late at night hoist a
horse (yes, a horse) into the church belfry in
St. Marys along with some hay tied to the
church bell? Because when the horse went
to eat the hay, he rang the church bell, which drew the towns-
people to see the strange sight and wonder how they would get
the horse down again. That gave the smugglers enough time to
land some contraband at the dock, unobserved by the local
residents, who were gawking at a horse in a belfry. That 1808
church, a Union Church where all denominations could worship, would later become the First Presbyterian Church.

    One of the oldest towns in Georgia is St. Marys, locat-
ed in Camden County in the southeastern part of the state
about nine miles from the Atlantic Ocean. Its earliest inhabitants may have been the Timucuan tribe, who are said to have
been ruled by a beautiful queen.

    The nearby St. Marys River, which forms the border
with Florida, had several Indian names that were difficult for
white settlers to pronounce: Thlathlthlagupka, Flaflagafga,
and Slafea-Gufea. And the Indian names meant something

like "rotten or stinking fish," which was not conducive to attracting more settlers.

In 1787, just four years after Spain regained control of Florida from England, a group of settlers paid $38 for 1,620 acres. They then planned the town of St. Marys as a depot from which they could ship the agricultural and timber products produced in the area. The man who sold the settlers the land was Jacob Weed, who himself had received huge land grants from Camden County as an incentive to settle there. The newcomers had to contend with the Native Americans, the Spanish, and the smugglers, but those problems evaporated when Florida became part of the United States in 1821. When it did, St. Marys lost its distinction of being the southernmost town in the United States.

St. Marys prospered as both a shipping port and as a shipbuilding center because of its proximity to the ocean. In 1808, as the residents settled in and began making plans for a house of worship, they built Union Church, the third oldest church in Georgia. Its first pastor, Reverend Horace Pratt and his wife, Jane, lived in the beautiful Greek Revival mansion, Orange Hall, across the street. In the huge house with its columned portico, the Pratts entertained many guests over the years. Orange Hall became one of the centers of the social life of the town. The verse over the fireplace is often quoted:

Happy is the home that shelters a friend.
O turn thy rudder thitherward awhile—
Here may the storm-beat vessel safely ryde!
This is the port of rest from troublous toyle—
The World's sweet Inn from pain and wearisome
    turmoyle.

The Union Church of horse-in-the-belfry fame became the Independent Presbyterian Church in 1828, and then the First Presbyterian Church of St. Marys in the Georgia Presbytery in 1832. Its basement also housed classes for a school called the "Old Academy." The future looked promising for the town.

But in the 1860s, the Civil War disrupted their lives in many ways. During the Civil War, the residents evacuated to the safety of an inland town. This was a good move, since federal gunboats shelled St. Marys. After the war, the railroad replaced ships as the way to transport lumber to markets, and St. Marys steadily declined. It got a new lease on life when it served as the seat of Camden County for fifty-two years (1871-1923), and again when a local pulp mill created jobs in the 1940s. The recent development of the nearby King's Bay Naval Submarine Base for Trident submarines, which is not open to the public, will also help the town, whose population has now grown to over eight thousand.

The Historic District of St. Marys includes the original town grid. The streets, which are still in the same pattern as originally plotted in 1788, memorialize in their names the founders of the town, for example, Bryant, Conyers, Dillingham, Osborne, and Weed. One unusual kind of marker in the Historic District is the number of signs in braille.

The District is bounded by Alexander and Norris Streets, Waterfront Road, and the Oak Grove Cemetery. The cemetery has among its many tombstones some with French inscriptions, recalling a time in the eighteenth century when French-speaking Acadians from Canada, immortalized in Henry Wadsworth Longfellow's poem "Evangeline," settled there. The cemetery has graves of soldiers from every war the United States has fought, and at least one entire family who were killed by yellow fever.

On the waterfront is the National Park Service building that arranges transportation to Cumberland Island. At Orange Hall, visitors can arrange for tours of the town to see places like the Captain Morse House and the Toonerville Trolley that used to carry passengers to Kingsland.

The visitors can also see the Washington Oak. This is the place where four trees were planted on the day that President George Washington was buried in 1799. That day, grieving residents of St. Marys went down to the dock, met a boat carrying a symbolic corpse of the president, took the casket up Osborne Street, and buried it where the oak stands today. The well nearby was dug the same year as Washington's burial and has been known as the "Washington Pump" ever since.

Near the Washington Oak is the Jackson-Clark-Bessent-MacDonnell House, which dates from around 1801. Its most famous owner was Major Archibald Clark, who served as collector for the port of St. Marys under nine presidents, beginning with Jefferson. When Clark first took up that position, St. Marys was the southernmost port in the United States and therefore of great importance.

One of Clark's many visitors was vice president Aaron Burr, the man who killed Alexander Hamilton in a duel. Burr had attended law school with Clark. Another of Clark's visitors was General Winfield Scott, commander of the United States Army.

East of St. Marys is the forgotten site of Fort Tonyn, a fortification on Point Peter that the British built in 1776 to try to control that part of Georgia during the American Revolution.

DIRECTIONS

St. Marys is east of I-95 on State Road 40. For more information about St. Marys call the tourism council at (912) 882-4000 or 800-868-8687, or write to them at P.O. Box 1291, St. Marys, GA 31558.

Further Reading

Georgia Writers' Project. *Drums and Shadows: Survival Studies among the Georgia Coastal Negroes.* Athens, GA: University of Georgia Press, 1986, pp. 186–194: "St. Marys."

Burnette Vanstory. *Georgia's Land of the Golden Isles.* Athens, GA: University of Georgia Press, 1956, esp. pp. 192–200.

∽ Conclusion

*I*n May of 1997, just before I finished this book, my family and I were on Jekyll Island, preparing for a day of biking. It was late at night. We had just come from a dock on the northern tip of the island where we could see in the distance the light from St. Simons Lighthouse. Several boats were heading out for a night of fishing. A few anglers were trying their luck in the changing tide. Distant Brunswick was settling in for the night.

Along the bike path we saw two deer calmly nibbling some grass and eyeing some flowers near one of the houses. The deer looked up at us, probably wondering why we were intruding on their world. And then they resumed their nightly repast, oblivious to us. Nearby were the ruins of an eighteenth-century tabby house that had fallen to the ravages of time and weather. A mile away were the mansions, euphemistically called "cottages" by the northern millionaires who once hunted on the island.

The contrast of that scene has stayed with me. Georgia has so much natural beauty, combined with a history that goes back hundreds, even thousands, of years. I realize that Tybee, St. Simons, Sea, and Jekyll are developed and very popular with vacationers and full-time residents. But coastal Georgia also has St. Catherines, Blackbeard, Ossabaw, and Cumberland, almost totally devoid of human habitation. If anything, they have become less developed, less inhabited in the last hundred years.

If you have the time and inclination as you head north or south along I-95, consider meandering along the coastal route, near the tidal marshes, through the small towns. You will see forts and plantations and lighthouses and churches that will astound you. Well done, Georgians. You have managed to preserve many of your coastal historic sites, while at the same time keeping in a natural condition your unexcelled sea islands. For that, the rest of us are grateful.

⚡ Index

The Florida Keys: A History of the Pioneers by John Viele. As vividly portrayed as if they were characters in a novel, the true-life inhabitants of the Florida Keys will capture your admiration as you share in the dreams and realities of their daily lives.

Guardians of the Lights by Elinor De Wire. Stories of the men and women of the U.S. Lighthouse Service. In a charming blend of history and human interest, this book paints a colorful portrait of the lives of a vanished breed.

Guide to Florida Lighthouses by Elinor De Wire. Its lighthouses are some of Florida's oldest and most historic structures, with diverse styles of architecture and daymark designs.

Key Biscayne: A History of Miami's Tropical Island and the Cape Florida Lighthouse by Joan Gill Blank. This is the engaging biography of the southernmost barrier island in the United States and the Cape Florida Lighthouse that has stood at its southern tip for 170 years.

Legendary Islands of the Ocean Sea by Robert H. Fuson. From the diaries and charts of early explorers comes the intriguing story of the real and imagined islands of what we now know as the Atlantic and Pacific Oceans.

Lighthouses of Ireland by Kevin M. McCarthy with paintings by William L. Trotter. Eighty navigational aids under the authority of the Commissioners of Irish Lights dot the two thousand miles of Irish coastline. Each is addressed here, and thirty of the most interesting ones are featured with detailed histories and full-color paintings.

Lighthouses of the Carolinas by Terrance Zepke. Eighteen lighthouses aid mariners traveling the coasts of North and South Carolina. Here is the story of each, from origin to current status, along with visiting information and photographs.

Search for the Great Turtle Mother by Jack Rudloe with illustrations by Marty Capron. Intrigued by turtle legends from many cultures, Rudloe travels the globe observing the silent rituals of sea turtles and learns timeless lessons about conservation and respect for the earth.

Shipwrecks of Florida: A Comprehensive Listing by Steven D. Singer. General information on research, search and salvage, wreck identification, artifact conservation, and rights to wrecks accompanies a listing of 2100 wrecks off the Florida coast from the sixteenth century to the present.

The Spanish Treasure Fleets by Timothy R. Walton. The story of how the struggle to control precious metals from Spain's colonies in Latin America helped to shape the modern world.

Thirty Florida Shipwrecks by Kevin M. McCarthy with paintings by William L. Trotter. Sunken treasure, prison ships, Nazi submarines, and the Bermuda triangle make what the *Florida Historical Quarterly* calls "exciting history."

Twenty Florida Pirates by Kevin M. McCarthy with paintings by William L. Trotter. Notorious Florida pirates from the 1500s to the present include Sir Francis Drake, Black Caesar, Blackbeard, and José Gaspar — not to mention present-day drug smugglers.